PRIVATE GARDENS

Design Secrets to Creating Beautiful Outdoor Living Spaces

First reprinted 2022
The Images Publishing Group Reference Number: 1663

First published in Australia in 2019 by
The Images Publishing Group Pty Ltd
ABN 89 059 734 431

Offices

Melbourne
6 Bastow Place
Mulgrave, Victoria 3170
Australia
Tel: +61 3 9561 5544

New York
6 West 18th Street 4B
New York, NY 10011
United States
Tel: +1 212 645 1111

Shanghai
6F, Building C, 838 Guangji Road
Hongkou District, Shanghai 200434
China
Tel: +86 021 31260822

books@imagespublishing.com
www.imagespublishing.com

NATIONAL LIBRARY OF AUSTRALIA
A catalogue record for this book is available from the National Library of Australia

Title: Private Gardens: Design Secrets to Creating Beautiful Outdoor Living Spaces
Author: Kurt Schaus (introductory text)
ISBN: 9781864708462

Printed by Toppan Excel (Dongguan) Printing CO,. LTD.

IMAGES has included on its website a page for special notices in relation to this and its other publications. Please visit www.imagespublishing.com

Contents

Kurt Schaus

Principal Designer of R. Youngblood & Co.

A graduate from Michigan State University, with a degree in Landscape Horticulture with a focus on design, Kurt Schaus—Principal Designer of R. Youngblood & Co. (founded by Ryan Youngblood, Principal, in 1997)—has heightened the levels of all projects he's been involved with since joining the firm in 2005. Known for his ability to conceptualize a landscape plan that harmonizes with proven install specifications, he's adept at overcoming site challenges and functionally serves the desired vision and lifestyle requirements of clients. With a strong understanding of the relationship between site, architecture, and environment, Kurt effectively prioritizes the project scope to the most desirable outcome. He serves the firm and its clients greatly with his 30 years of experience and the understanding of what is behind the making of a garden. His role and abilities have allowed R. Youngblood & Co. to be the proud recipient of awards for garden design and excellence on several occasions.

Foreword

Typically, a private garden is thought to be a personal expression of an accomplished designer's abilities where one is encouraged to let their passion be expressed to the fullest without worry of the treasures created within being stolen and duplicated elsewhere. Certainly, there are some designers who look at garden design from this point of view, but the truth is something far more simple and, yet, extremely more complicated to achieve at the same time.

To understand the development of private gardens, one must accept that there is no classroom or publication in print that can explain how approaching such a project is accomplished. It is a long journey that is ignited in those who begin to pursue a passion for garden design. Beginning with, first, the study of plants and the wonder of all their characteristics, this knowledge then needs to be combined with a solid understanding of the mathematics of geometry and the use of scale and the relationship of proportions.

The earliest years are spent learning raw function and putting it together to develop working concepts. From these, landscape designers must progress on to developing a style that fits a designer's personality while, at the same time, expanding the vision for each landscape. This is the point where talent blossoms and the road forks. Some continue to polish the individual style they've developed and become the very best at that; developing a strong reputation, they become content with what they have achieved. The other fork shows how much more there is to appreciate and learn in the field of landscape gardens and leads to the next step: the world of landscape philosophy.

The philosophy of design instructs the designer to take the years of experience and knowledge gained and put them to work structuring a vision for the garden that the recipient would have had, if only they had the insight. The private garden has so much more to offer when it takes a foreign space, manipulates what it has to use there, and transforms it into a singularly personal environment for the enjoyment of its host. Any space crafted with some thought toward design can yield a beautiful garden, but it falls short of the ability to reach out and touch the soul of the individual for whom the garden was intended.

Consider the purchase of an engagement ring. You may find something suitable in a jeweler's case but to have an expert jeweler handcraft the perfect setting makes it all the more desirable and treasured. Similarly, what is required from a private garden is a space that feeds off the desires of the host, crafted by a designer that can absorb all that is seen and heard from the client to form a vision for the space that is intimately personal and rewarding.

Where the face of a home or property is the simplest expression of landscape on a structure, designed to work with the architecture and environment of the residence to create excitement and appeal for spectators as they

pass by the property, the backyard, in stark contrast, is the expression of those who dwell within it. It considers, as most important, the deepest desires of the occupants and how they choose to live, the endless memories they intend to build, and the enjoyment they expect from the property they have selected to call home.

This is the space seldom shown to the public and, in fact, from the street can seem almost empty and void of activity. In truth, this area is often intentionally kept secret, for private use only. It houses every family event and celebration—from the first swing-set to cookouts and birthdays, even raising the family dog and providing a final resting place. It is in use from the earliest light of dawn to well past twilight for quiet gatherings around an open flame or the activity surrounding a pool.

A passion for the private garden drives the designer to search out ideas, perhaps outside of the normal comfort zone, to fulfil the desires for the private garden itself. To express this thought, think of how to approach the design vision for a traditional colonial-style home set in the suburban neighborhood. This is instantly conceivable to most designers. It's not so simple when you think of placing that same home into a thickly wooded mountain lot, or under the wide open sky of a desert landscape.

It is at this point that individual style either agrees with the chosen site and home placed there and continues on to complete a garden concept, or walks away in disgust because the whole precept of placing the home in this location is just wrong. The missing element here is understanding why someone would want the home built in this location. Landscape philosophy requires you to make that connection. The challenge is to make the commitment to grasp and understand what must happen to the vision for the home and grounds in any environment so that the home feels as though it belongs and its appeal is inviting and welcoming.

You must accomplish the goal in a way that is beyond question to all those who would judge the end result, while still completing the vision in a way that connects the garden intimately with the intended participant. Every detail is important and must be considered for the development of the concept in mind. Not only the shape of the walkway but also the materials selected for use in each environment should bring the vision together. The orientation of the patio and how it the affects the view combined with the layering of garden to maximize the use of space while connecting to the surrounding environment is also essential.

Consideration for the passage of time also plays a role that needs to be understood in the private garden, which will be displayed daily through movement of the wind and the track of the sun, as well as seasonally from the spring awakening to the winter hibernation. If all of these can be accomplished, the garden not only suits the owner but becomes a timeless treasure for many generations to follow. Thus begins the story of the private garden.

It seems only natural that the origins and development of the private garden follows a similar path to the garden designer. Driven purely out of necessity, the garden should have established boundaries and limits to keep the encroachments at bay. These barriers also served to control Mother Nature, deter the ravages of flooding and ercsion, and shield from the wind.

This framework, while functional and necessary, entraps the space and can make even the largest of areas seem small and confined. A creative approach with the insight to grasp at the understanding of how these spaces could be transformed into garden environments was at the beginnings of private garden development. The culture of the local people and esthetics of the region gave rise to the style that would be expressed in the garden and polished over time, would begin to define a region, and would place a historical marker for that place and time.

The approach to developing a space into a private garden takes many differing directions based on what the owners' wishes are for the space and the influences of the designer. For some, the intent is that the entire garden is to be viewed and experienced all at once from a chosen vantage point. To view a garden in this manor is like witnessing the impact of a drop of water on the surface of glassy smooth pond and observing the ripples spreading out across the limits of the pond's dimension and interacting with any obstacle encountered on its path.

Devising a crosswalk that would not upset the symmetry of the garden, while providing access, is difficult but will aesthetically connect the garden space together into one cohesive vista from the view above. In addition to the functional features the pathway provides, it also invites exploration of the garden and reveals the hidden pleasure of sightlines to an accent piece or destination through the space. This feature has to be experienced and can only be appreciated from within the garden itself. It remains inconspicuously hidden from the vantage point view of the garden from above.

Other approaches look at the garden as a journey that is to be revealed only in bits and pieces as one travels along the way. The limitations of the garden development

should disappear into the background as the garden is slowly revealed around the epicenter, without exposing what was anticipated to be there until the journey's end. Thus, the journey can build in excitement, drawing the traveler on in anticipation of what might be found further along, the pace quickening as the destination is approached and the awaiting interior is revealed.

Another approach is that of designing the garden as one would the interior of a home. Starting with a kind of entrance foyer, the garden design can draw people in, as though down a hallway, to spaces designated to each specific purpose, such as a pool area, a recreation area, and an open courtyard with a stone fireplace, table, and seating inviting people to relax. This intentionally blurs the line of what is house and what is yard, embracing the use and enjoyment of being outdoors.

Ignoring all of these concepts might lead to an approach where one harmonizes with the surroundings, such as utilizing the stone cliff face on the side of the property as the back wall of the gathering space, set with large stone blocks as seating, and the natural lichen as carpet. Or creating a walkway that mimics a mountain stream cutting through the space and meandering back up to the residence, drawing the inhabitants to come out and partake in the natural environment. Such a setting is designed for several vantage points and no two of them reveal the same sightline or focal point. Interest is to be found in every corner as the perspective changes throughout the garden.

Deciding on how to approach the overall design concept from the many options available is only the beginning of the design process. A start could be made, for instance, with the front yard, seeing it as an extension of the home and using the architecture of the house as a guide. Form a space for the vantage point of the private garden, such as a terrace or patio that is an extension of the residence utilizing the architectural features of the home. Observe the space that has been created and consider where the views should be directed and what needs to be screened. Connect the space to the yard beyond to provide open access to the yard and gardens, as well as traffic flow from and around the home. Now consider how the layout affects the views from inside the home, taking into account the importance that these features have on the time spent dwelling within and from season to season.

Many details are driven by architecture and its application in the private garden. A contemporary home would easily lend itself to a broken-edge patio with a walkway leading out past garden beds massed with grasses. But under the influence of the designer, the details of the layout can be manipulated to achieve the direction the designer wants to accomplish. Simply altering how a broken-edge shape is formed can transform it from bold contemporary to clean minimalist or even symmetrically traditional. Either one would work well with the suggested architecture of the home but the influence in the details establish the desired outcome for the design direction intended.

The selection of materials used in construction is also a detail that influences the outcome of its design. In our sample contemporary home with broken-edge patio and walkways, consider how the use of plain white concrete would look versus large multicolored pieces of random irregular flagstone. Much depends on location.

One approach would be right at home in an upscale suburban development while the other requires a rocky desert landscape with tufted clumps of natural grasses and a mountainous backdrop.

Next, consider accessorizing the vision with accents and focal interest, such as the implementation of large angular stone outcrops chunked in along the pathway versus stout masonry columns spotted along the way adorned with planters for seasonal color. Slabs of antiqued granite curbing set slightly higher than the pavement accentuate and expand the limits of the broken-edge design, while a precisely cut rectangular medallion of finished marble inserted into the patio can designate a dining location.

Consideration for how details influence the direction of the garden's design is important to understand when attempting to meet or exceed expectations. Influences come from the local culture, religion or beliefs, location of being urban or rural, and historic or modern. They are further driven through travel experience by outside cultures such as French, English, or Mediterranean and by regions like tropical island, rainforest, Icelandic coast, and alpine mountain, just to name a few examples.

Outside cultures can have a dramatically different approach to the implementation of the same garden concept. Just consider fabrics and the variety of patterns alone from all over the world and one begins to understand the vast range of influence to be had

on garden design and individual desires. It is for this reason that the passionate garden designer has to understand and appreciate all forms of design and be open to exploring many options when designing a private garden for an equally passionate client. Only then will you experience the satisfaction of providing a singularly personal environment that is capable of touching the soul of the individual for whom the garden was intended.

The gardens of a home are an important element in creating an inviting living place for the residents. Of such importance are gardens that they can transform an unassuming, plain space into a very desirable and habitable environment. By the same token, done wrong, they can mask the true beauty of an incredible home, causing visitors to walk by unimpressed. Many people feel they have a true gift in the ability to critique a garden as beautifully conceived and constructed or done horribly wrong and showing lack of talent.

The truth is that even the average spectator can decide if a garden is beautiful or not. If a garden is done well it is appreciated by all—even if they don't necessarily understand it—and people can enjoy the experience of the space. If something is out of place or ill conceived, the only thing that is obvious to all is that something is not right. It requires a trained eye and a great deal of understanding, with time invested in working with outdoor spaces, to identify the root cause of an abstraction in the garden. Once identified and corrected, the accomplishments of the garden space should flourish and become appealing to all once again, with the average spectator never quite grasping how or why.

While studying the private gardens of others it is important to understand that these gardens were designed to suit the clients and provide a glimpse of what, personally, makes them happy in their homes. Some use the space to unwind and relax at the end of a long day, such as a doctor who deals with death on a daily basis and is looking for replenishment of the soul to be able to recharge to continue work the next day. Others require excitement and the joy of being alive and the need to share their space to create and strengthen bonds with friends and family on a daily basis. It is important to know and keep in mind as you study these gardens that when the intent of these private gardens is understood, the space takes on a whole new meaning and appreciation. Each private garden was designed with a purposeful intent for the user and says as much about the inhabitant as it does about the space created for them to use, which is a secluded sanctuary for personal enjoyment for some and an expansive entertaining area for others.

These spaces are to be judged on the moods they create for the space they were envisioned in. Pay attention to the environments they have chosen to be placed in and the challenges or limits these environments have placed on the vision. In addition, note how the environment may have been used to the advantage of the design, pushing the limits of what was accomplished by way of creating a singularly usable space that could not have been matched anywhere else.

Try to identify the expectations of the project, and the fulfilment of those expectations by the garden space created. See if you can identify the personality or occupation of the resident, based on how the space is designed for use. Understanding these behind-the-scenes attributes may add to the appreciation of what is presented and may take off the blinders most people wear to allow a wider vision for what can be accomplished in a garden space, expanding the possibilities of what would have previously been acceptable or achievable in garden design and the pure enjoyment of what an outdoor environment can provide.

If you find yourself being drawn to some of the spaces in this book and wondering how these spaces could be achieved in your own private garden, our expectations have been achieved. Keep in mind that any space custom crafted to fulfill your desires with a single focus and vision will achieve its goal. Loss of this focused vision or influence from too many inspirations will lead to failure in accomplishing the vision for the garden and, hence, a loss of the passion for it. A single bold concept followed through with focused vision will ultimately provide much more enjoyment and a sense of accomplishment than the chaos caused by too many features.

Experience achieved through diligence and time is the only path that can ultimately make a true garden designer. Rewards that last a lifetime await the sojourner at the end of the journey but many lessons must be learned and put into practice so that what is presented in a vision for the garden are tried and true.

The Gardens

The Orchard Ridge Garden

R. Youngblood & Co.

Oakland County, Michigan, United States
87,000 square feet (8090 square meters)

Photography / Jeff Garland

In this project, the owner of the home wanted a residential estate with the feel of formal European gardens, as explored in their many travels. As such, the landscape was designed to remind the owner of their travels and the many gardens that inspired them.

The pool has a true infinity edge that dumps water into a lower trough. All edges of the pool were made flush with the bluestone pool terrace to give a seamless look to the water's edge. Both the spa and the in-pool fire bowl were treated with an infinity edge to allow a sleek, floating appearance. A local metal artist was commissioned to design and fabricate the copper fire bowl as well the wrought-iron garden arbors and gate.

The garden design included several traditional plant choices, including boxwood, hydrangea, roses, and several perennials. Two large hornbeam trees frame the sightline looking through the boxwood parterre garden and two custom garden arbors. Centering the sightline sits a garden cherub perfectly framed by purple climbing clematis.

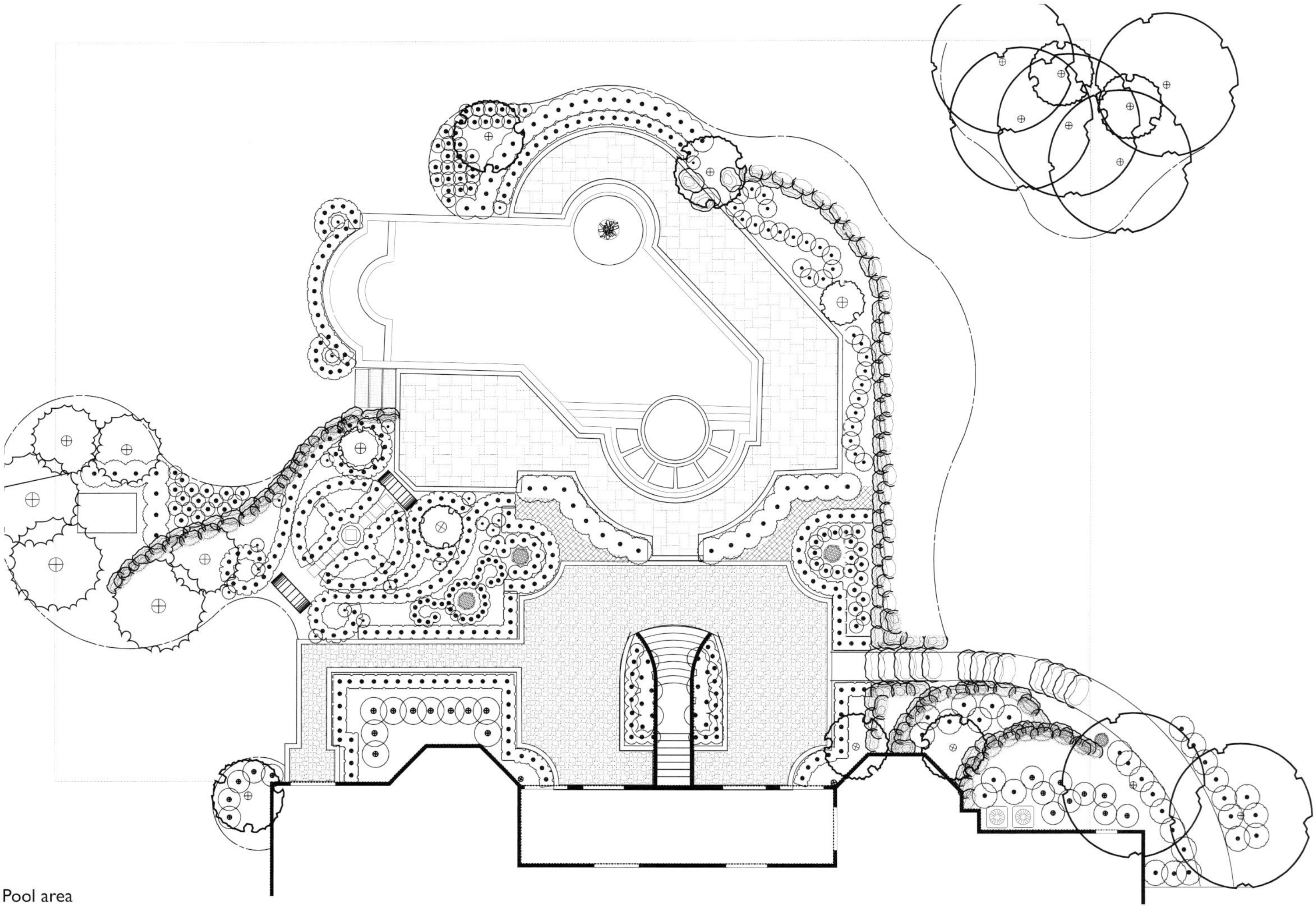

Pool area

Garden with a view

Bahl GmbH

The owners of this property located in Harmstorf, Germany wanted an outdoor-entertaining area with a swimming pool, alfresco lounge with kitchen and dining area, and numerous seating and resting options.

The designers decided to create a space with basic geometric forms and uniformity of plants, which came to characterize the garden. Beyond the house, which is framed by mature trees, the pre-existing birches and rhododendrons make a nice transition to the garden.

The prevailing flower colors in violet, pink, and white form a pleasant contrast against the patio tiles, the blue of the pool, and the green of the lawn and other plants. The garden was designed to be used late into the evening beside an outdoor fireplace.

Harmstorf, Germany

32,292 square feet (3000 square meters)

Planning office / G&B Gartendesign

Photography / Miquel Tres

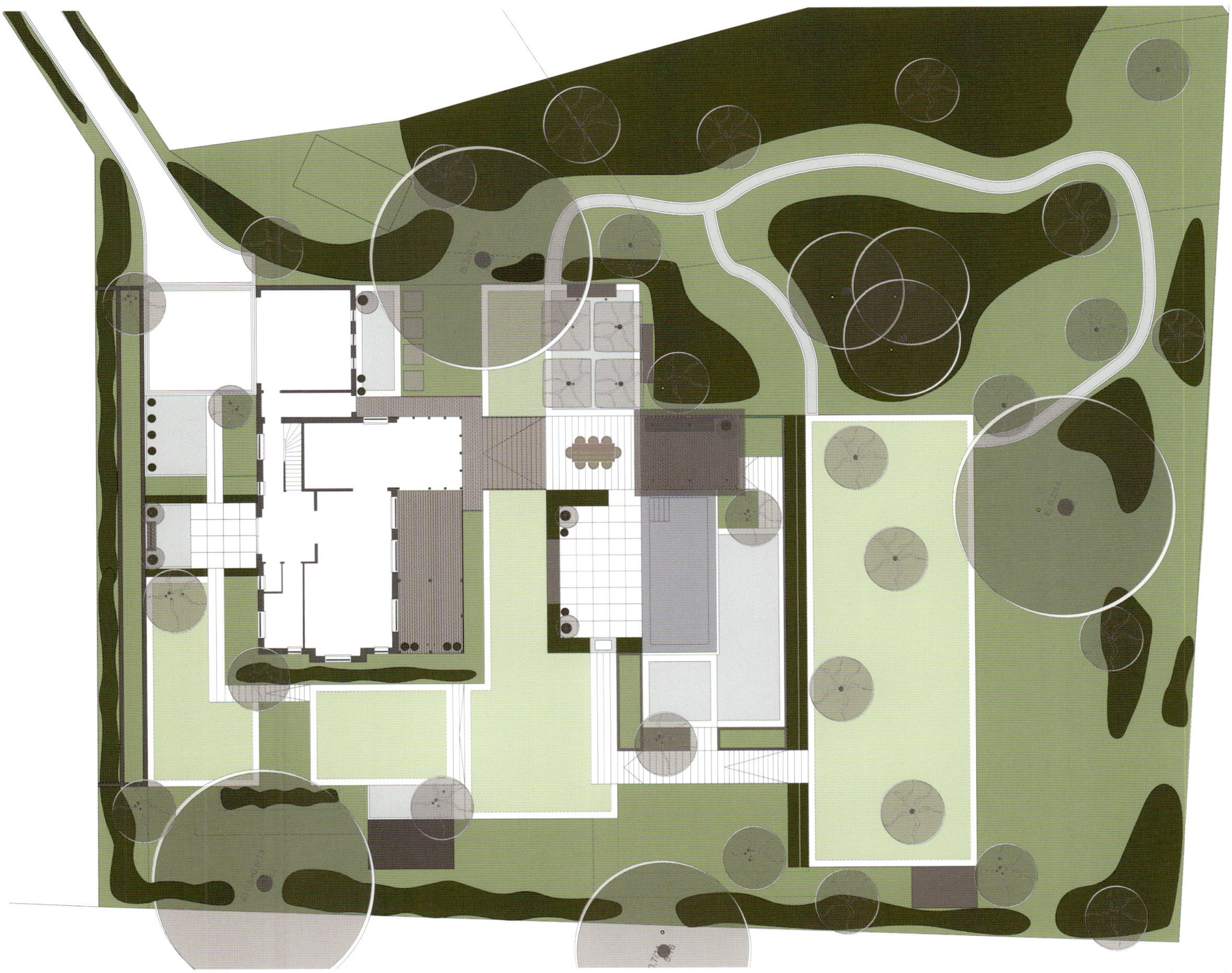

Master plan

Oakville Garden 2

Janet Rosenberg & Studio, Glenn Piotrowski Architect Ltd.

Oakville, Canada

10,465 square feet (972 square meters)

Photography / Jeff McNeill Photography

A daughter's wish for a garden party for her upcoming marriage spurred this project, which was quickly implemented through the skills of a contractor. Fortunately, mature and specimen trees already on-site offered the established setting of a peaceful country environment in this residential neighborhood within the Golden Horseshoe of southern Ontario.

The existing mature and specimen trees provided an instant landscape, reinforcing the timelessness of the classical elements in the design. Yet, new plantings of trees—with some being large established specimens—included Callery pear and hornbeam, while for shrubs and groundcover the choices included Green Velvet

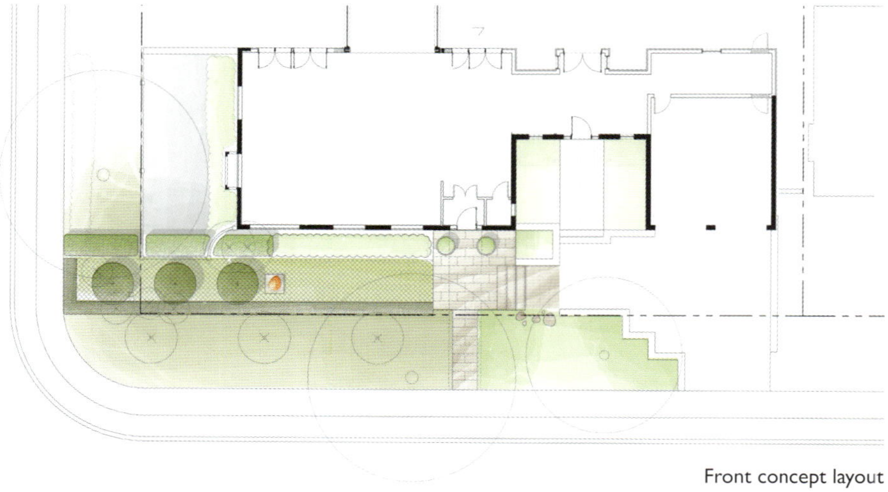

Front concept layout

Boxwoods, Hill's yew, and winter creeper. Views outward revealed this layered landscape's composition of elements stepping between the viewer and the background.

Meanwhile, the buffer of lawn along the property's perimeter provides the transitional step—and necessary proximity to the terrace—and helps identify the new intervention as a special precinct within the garden. The planter perimeter along the fence also creates a strong sense of privacy through the concept of a

transitional buffer space to the elevated garden terrace. Views outward to the perimeter and street illustrate the benefit of screening from planting within, in addition to reinforcing the edge.

Clients are always drawn to the potential desirability of reflective ponds as a design element. Algonquin limestone provides an elegant setting for the outdoor dining terrace, unifying the materials of the home with the water feature and garden.

As collectors of modern art, the couple brought their architecture and interior design training to bear to favor a contemporary edginess on the design of a classical retreat. In the end, their choice to install the sculpture *Skinny Skull* (2014) by John McEwen at the garden focal point provides a critical counterpoint to the timeless vocabulary of terraces, planting beds, and ponds with flowing basins.

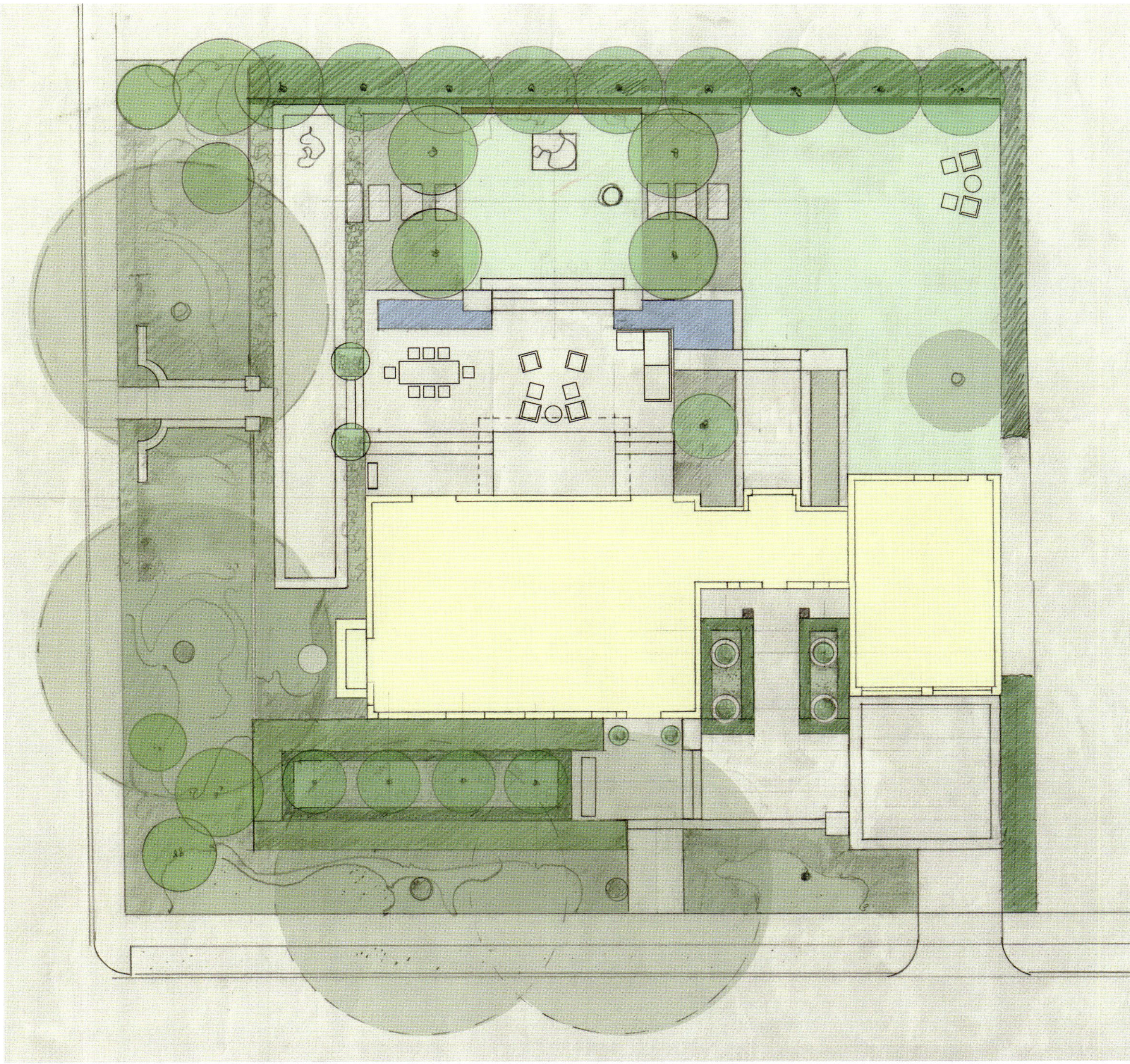

Sketch

A forest garden for a friend

Atelier Flera

A mid-size garden on the outskirts of Prague utilized the location to blend with the surrounding scenery. This concept makes the garden look much larger and embraces the surrounding nature and nearby forest.

The concept worked with two different aspects of the garden—light and shadows. In the southern part, the original forest has its own intimate atmosphere, while the main area is dominated by original coniferous trees with delicate underbrush flowers. The self-binding gravel pathway leads, via the forest, to the center of the garden, providing access to a modern wooden homestead. The clearing of vegetation was limited in order to embrace the natural surroundings.

The natural format of the landscape sought to fulfill the potential of space, complemented by simple facilities—a fireplace, swing, seesaw, and sand pit for children, along with several raised garden beds designed for self-sufficient vegetable cultivation.

Prague, Czech Republic
10,010 square feet (930 square meters)

Photography / Atelier Flera

The main feature of the outdoor living area is a large patio terrace, which can be covered by a marquee. A massive oak staircase extends the whole space to connect the patio with the backyard. A stone wall compensates the split level of the land and can also be used as an occasional sitting area. A small washbasin further adds to the original concept and feel. A wood-storage facility provides functionality and privacy to the terrace area.

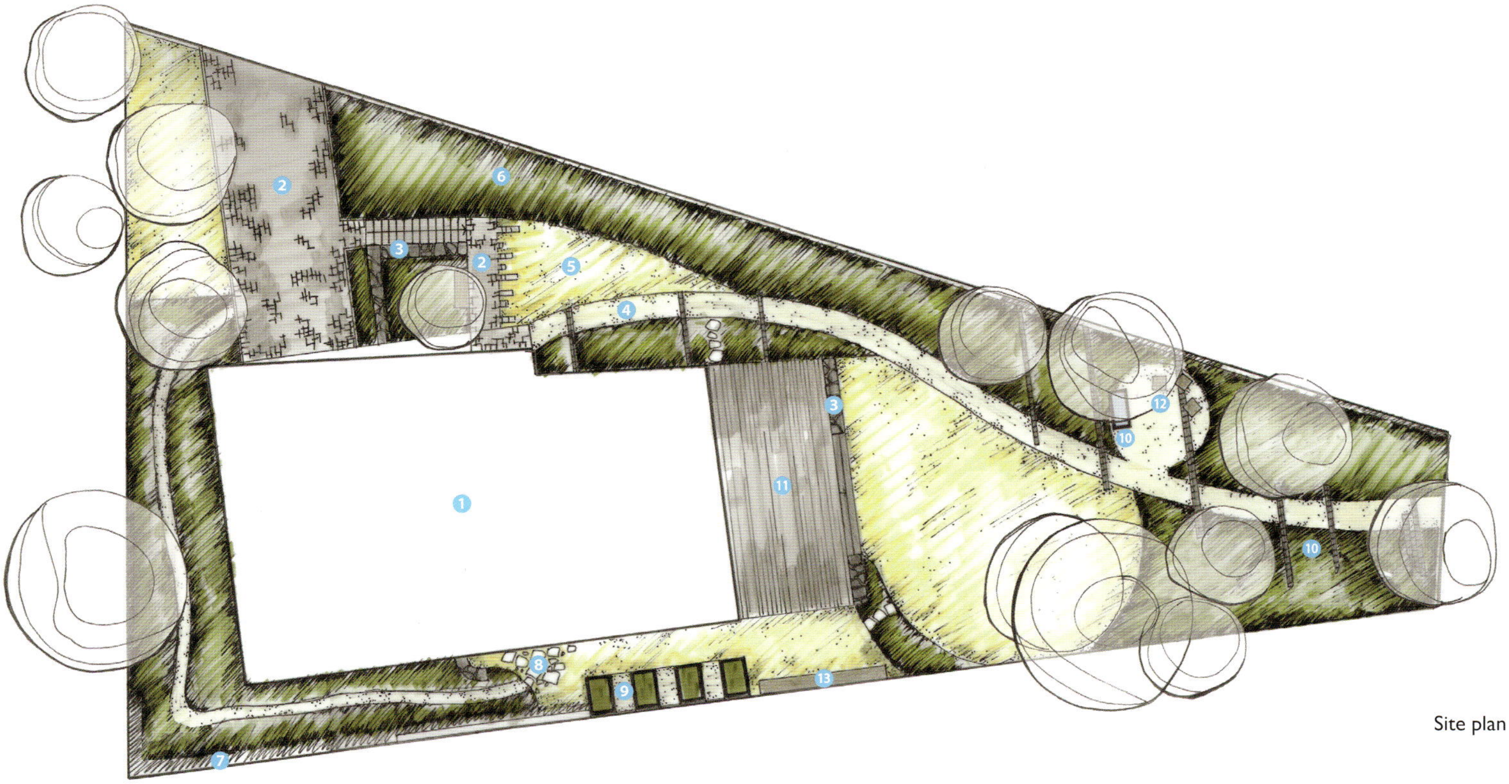

Site plan

1. House
2. Driveway and sidewalk
3. Dry stone walls
4. Granite road
5. Sod
6. Planting area
7. Quickset hedge
8. Stone tread
9. High-rise vegetable parterre
10. Basin
11. Wooden terrace
12. Bonfire
13. Wooden house

A narrow path around the house was lined with wild flowers and grass. Every nook of the garden was created to offer an opportunity to relax. Drinking fountains and feeders further encapsulate the coexistence with local wildlife.

Manor on the Baltic Sea

Bahl GmbH

Steinbergkirche, Schleswig-Holstein, Germany
538,196 square feet (50,000 square meters)

Planning office / Sebastian Jensen Hamburg
Photography / Miquel Tres, Torsten Scherz

This project saw the restoration of a lovely courtyard with a thatched roof into a huge garden area. Crafted in several stages, the design incorporated 150-year-old oak trees and a magnificent lime tree avenue, which was built 20 years ago and lines a 328-foot-long (100-meter-long) driveway.

Before the transformation, the garden was designed as a cottage garden with lots of boxwood, which was

incorporated into the hilly meadows and agricultural land around the garden area. The owners wanted a low-maintenance garden with plenty of seating for entertaining friends.

The renovated garden has many areas: a fruit and herb garden and large seating areas, as well as classic elements, such as an ornamental pond with a bronze figure. Existing art and decorative objects were integrated into the garden design. From the wooden deck, a wonderful view is framed over the wide space of the lake, which was once a wet meadow, and the adjoining area. The area by the water is graded with carefully designed *Friesenwällen* (small, rustic walls build out of thick stones), which are typical for this region.

Materials from the region (wood, sandstone slabs, granite, and boulders) form a unique garden with plants, water surfaces, planters, and art. The focus for the garden was on plants from the region, such as yew trees, plane trees, beech hedge, apple trees, pear, hydrangeas, roses, and perennials.

Site plan

Inviting nature

Art & Jardins Conception

In this garden located in Boucherville, Canada, the designers gave movement to the flowerbeds as well as to the stone path. Beautiful troughs filled in part with alpine plants line the path and accompany the walker. Spaces of green lawn were nicely cut from large masses of plants.

The designers played with textures and foliage colors. The volume of plants was also punctuated in places of interest. The curves harmonize naturally as if the natural forms of places were reflected in the sinuous shapes of materials and flowerbeds.

Aspiring to create a space where nature and the structures mix harmoniously, for the façade, they had to construct the gardens from scratch from the virgin ground, as it didn't have any trees or lawn. The stone paths, the low walls, and the plantations themselves promote a pleasant flow directed towards the entrance of the house.

Boucherville, Canada

16,146 square feet (1500 square meters)

Photography / Jean-Claude Hurni

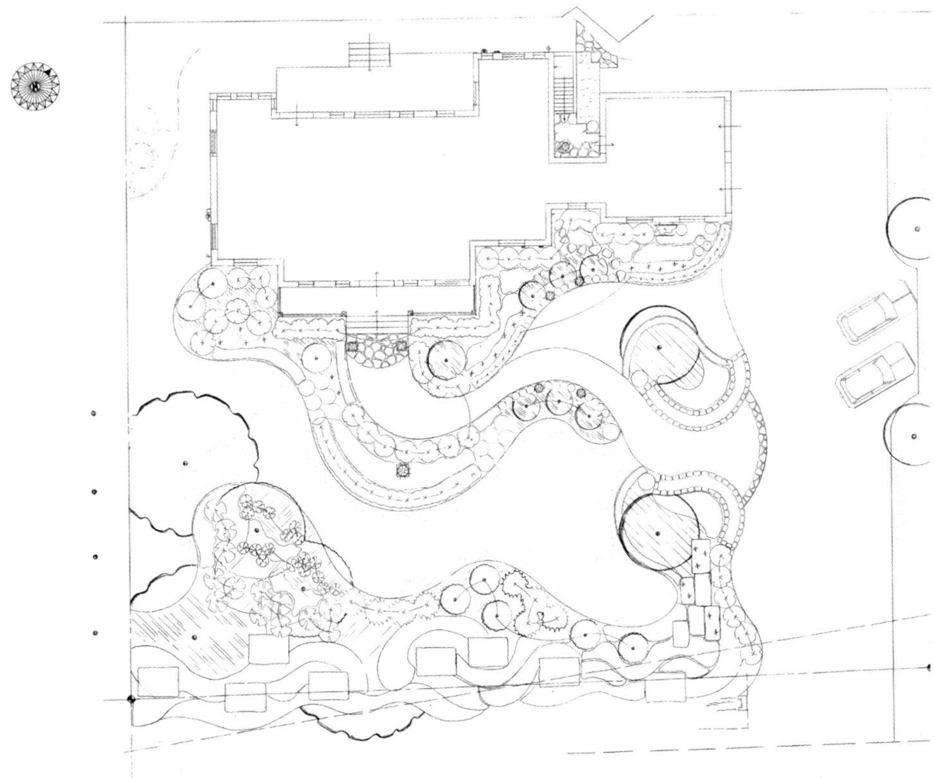

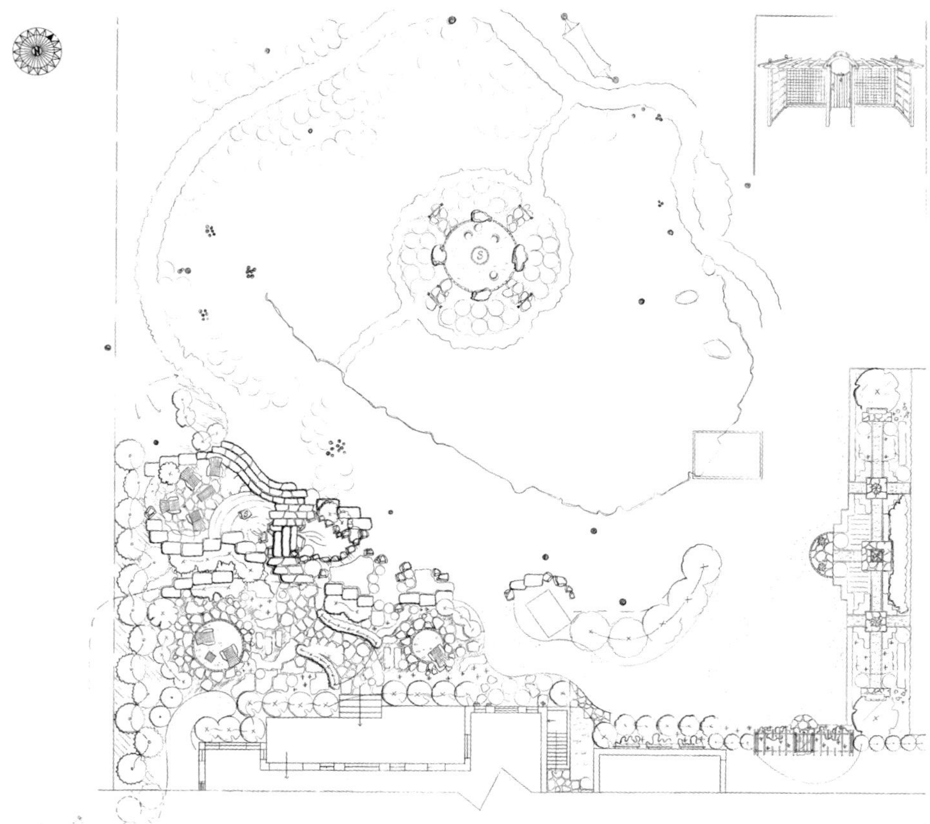

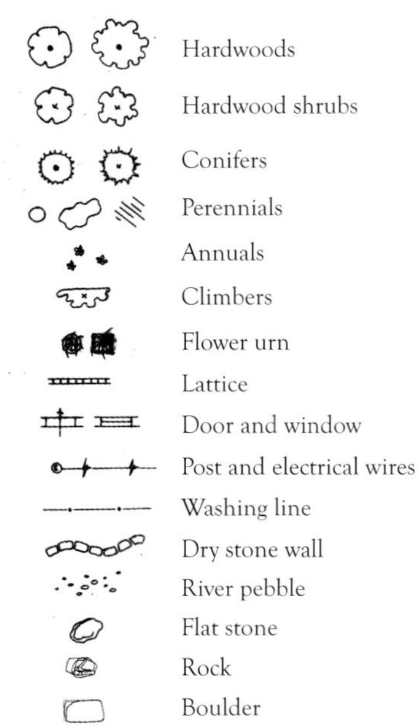
Hardwoods
Hardwood shrubs
Conifers
Perennials
Annuals
Climbers
Flower urn
Lattice
Door and window
Post and electrical wires
Washing line
Dry stone wall
River pebble
Flat stone
Rock
Boulder

Site plans

City villa in Hamburg's Harvestehude

Bahl GmbH

Hamburg, Germany

4306 square feet (400 square meters)

Planning office / Sebastian Jensen Hamburg

Photography / Peter Greitzke

After renovating this beautiful old Hamburg city villa in an Art Nouveau style, the garden was to be redesigned. The desire of the owners was a classic and noble design within the small property. The fact that the garden offers a lot of private space, despite its size, is due to the skillful selection of plants and the clear structure.

In one corner of the oval lawn, a wooden teahouse with a big window area and slate roof was built, allowing a green outdoor living space to be enjoyed, even in changing weather. Screen protectors to the neighboring house offer birch (*Betula utilis*), the white bark of which stands out beautifully from the oval planted yew hedge

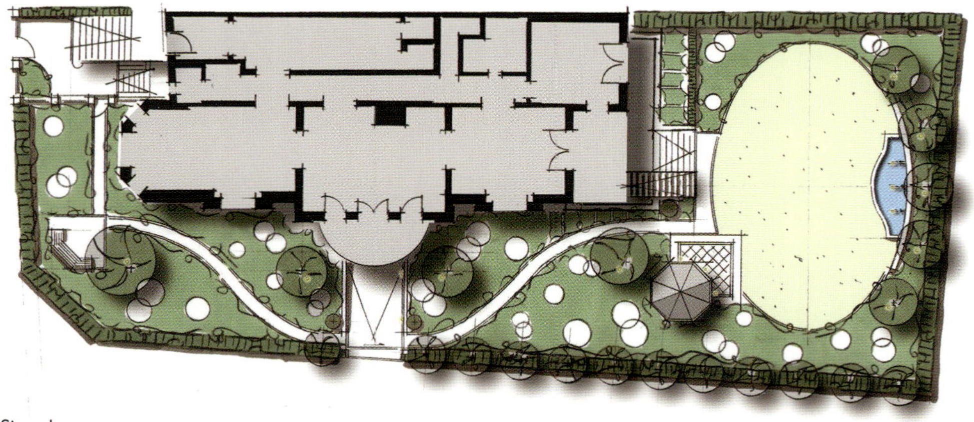

Site plan

An eye-catcher is the historic sandstone pool, which was imported from France. From two ancient sprues, water flows into the 300-year-old basin and soothes with its splashing. At a distance, two bronze rose sculptures are visible. All paths and squares are basalt, resuming the color black of the railings and windows of the house. Podiums and steps were made out of sandstone and emphasize the exclusivity of the object.

White-flowered hydrangeas, azaleas, and roses, as well as rhododendrons and *Allium* with violet flowers, set beautiful color accents to the yews and boxwood. The attractiveness of yew trees is on display in the garden with the spherical shape repeated in many areas. A large floral dogwood in the back garden and a red Japanese maple tree in the front area set beautiful color accents.

Numerous attractive seating areas make it possible to experience the garden with its clear forms. The uniformity of the materials and plants used with individual accents of water and art conveys harmony and security.

The Fridolin garden

Art & Jardins Conception

Saint-Bruno-de-Montarville, Canada
4736 square feet (440 square meters)
Photography / Jean-Claude Hurni

The clients aspired to create an outdoor space that would allow them to entertain friends and enjoy gardening in a lovely environment, while also providing a beautiful view from the interior of the home.

Responding to the clients' expectations, the designers used a good variety of materials. A welcoming façade made of natural stone matching the house and gravel paths leading to a garden courtyard. Within this space is an outdoor kitchen area, herb garden, and an inviting patio to entertain friends and relax outdoors, which also bolsters the appeal of the home.

The sculpture, *Fridolin* by Ménard-Biron, is the mascot of the home and the spirit of the garden.

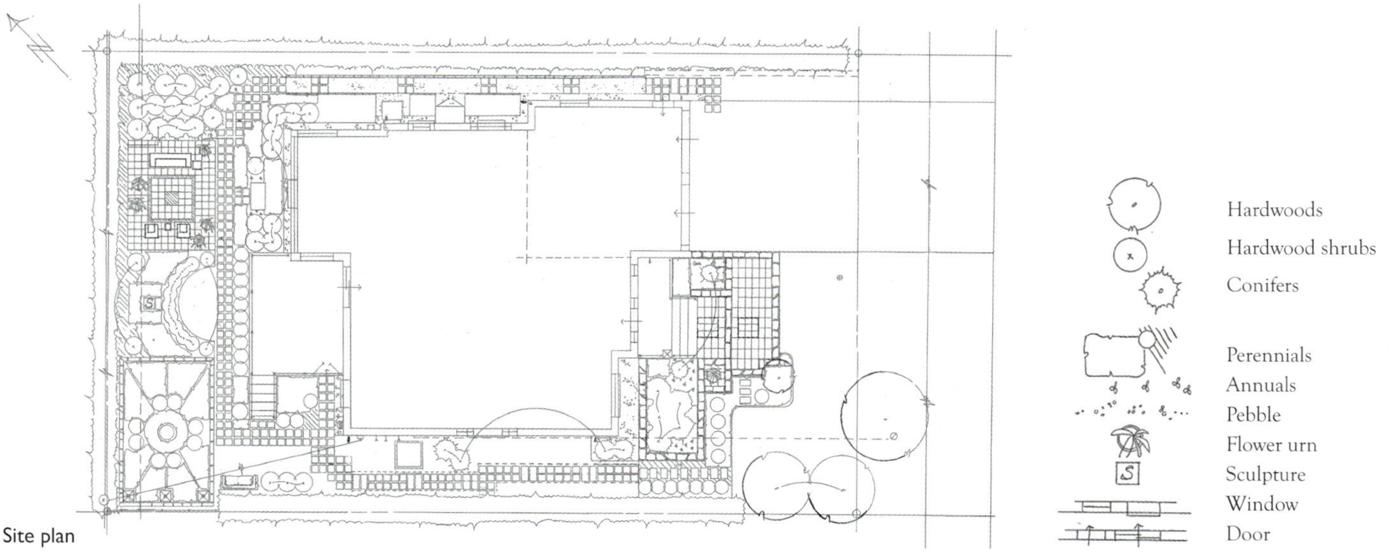

Site plan

Our First Home, Our First House

Nilufer Danis at Lotus Design Studio

London, United Kingdom
431 square feet (40 square meters)

Photography / Nilufer Danis & RHS

This gold-medal-winning and best "Low Cost, High Impact" garden was designed for a young professional couple with a small budget of £7000 to inspire a love of gardening and also allow for informal gatherings with friends as an outdoor room. The design used a sustainable and low-carbon-footprint approach, using reclaimed scaffold boards, recycled ceramic gravel, and a salvaged part from a Ford Model T as a sculpture.

Site plan

The key features of this project were: sustainable reclaimed scaffold boards used for walls, steps, and decking and recycled sanitary crushed ceramic used as a gravel surface within the sunken area. The salvaged part from a Ford Model T used as a sculpture creates visual intrigue, while the contemporary sunken seating area with chimenea and log store is ideal for entertaining.

The trees and shrubs selected provide wildlife habitat and evergreen shrubs create year-round structure. Colourful herbaceous planting looks most attractive during the summer barbecue season, which is just what the clients wanted.

Garden with the cat

Atelier Flera

A young couple who built an elegant modern home in a satellite town longed for more contact with nature. They wanted a pleasing minimalist environment with views of the surrounding countryside. Unconcerned by large trees, the designers were able to shield areas with solitaire oak and multi-maple directly on the terrace.

The whole site is bordered by a shaped hornbeam fence that provides privacy. Two circular lawns were designed in the garden. The lawn in the southern part is higher maintenance, while the northern grassy area is reminiscent of a meadow—and also hides the inground trampoline, thanks to a decreased need for mowing.

Nymburk, Czech Republic
8988 square feet (835 square meters)

Photography / Atelier Flera

Sketch

The landscapes were inspired by local natural communities to provide pine forests on sand with the representation of heath species. As such, some of the beds were mulched with sand. The landscape was created with several forms of vegetation that create organic shapes in the different geometric skeletons of the garden. There are almost monocultural grasslands that complement the white flowering perennial beds; other areas under the trees were planted with undergrowth types of herbs.

The landscaping was complemented by stripes of technical elements—trench paths, woodcutters, and massive oak benches, while also providing space for a hammock, shed, fireplace, and vegetable garden.

Country house

A. J. Miller Landscape Architecture

New York, United States
52,992 square feet (4923 square meters)

Photography / Charles Wright and Mariane Wheatley-Miller

The designers were asked to create a garden for the clients, but first they had to address the existing gardens that had been overgrown for many years and were dominated by an unimaginative lawn and dreary planting beds. Many yew hedges and trees were taken down and the lawn and borders all received new top-soil and fertilizers to lay the way for all new plants. The designers began to design the structure for the garden including the hardscape, driveway, and plant-bed outlines.

The driveway for guest drop-off at the grand entrance of the home was also designed. This hardscape design element delineated allowable driving areas, with room to accommodate guests. Brick pavers line the walkways, encouraging a visual dialog between the house and landscape. The paths were outlined and finished with custom-granite accent strips. The designers wanted to create a garden to reflect the sophistication of the house and surrounding neighborhood. The planting design required the removal of several overgrown trees. This new light and open space allowed for the creation of formal outdoor garden rooms.

A wrought-iron metal archway leads the visitor from the parking garage and forecourt through the herb garden, which is used extensively by the client for culinary applications. Secondary garden pathways lined with gravel branch off in regular intervals from the main passage. A. J. Miller Landscape Architecture devised a large brick terrace for outdoor dining and relaxation; substantial limestone trough planters border this area. Every season the planters are adorned with lavish horticultural arrangements. A vista overlooking a formal parterre can be enjoyed from a bench at the edge of the terrace, which rests upon an elegant plinth and large limestone urn.

A second formal garden room is located on the side of the house near a small private seating terrace—an extension of the interior living room. Visitors can follow pathways from the terrace to the "Great Lawn" under an archway planted with purple and copper beech climbers. Scented perennials anchor the space under the arch. The Great Lawn was established by removing some overgrown trees while protecting an ancient English beech in the center of the landscape.

Greenfield Oldham garden

David Keegan Garden Design

Greenfield, United Kingdom
5425 square feet (504 square meters)

Photography / David Keegan

Located in a warm and temperate region of the United Kingdom, the clients desired a sophisticated space for outdoor entertaining and one that acted as an extension of the home. They also wanted some form of terrace for alfresco seating to catch the last rays of sun in the early evening.

The concept was to create a dwarf-pine dry riverbed garden to include a small terrace for a table and chairs. A new lollipop boundary fence was installed and painted in a pale apple green and fore planted with Photinia Red Robin to add year-round color, with a variety of dwarf pines and silver foliaged plants to add form, contour, and additional color. An old chimney pot from the house was salvaged and used as a focal point. The clients were at first skeptical of this concept—not knowing how it would look—but loved it upon completion.

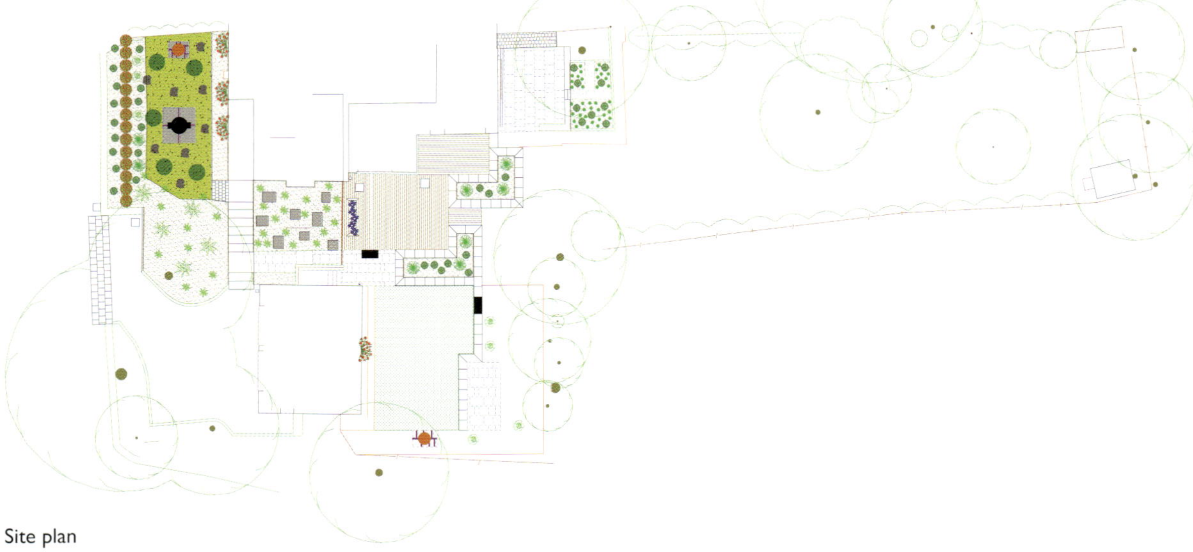

Site plan

Distinctly themed garden areas draw the focus into the space. Natural stone walls with stone copings created a dining space and connect the house to the gardens. A new boundary fence demarcates the gardens and offers more privacy.

Maples, *Alliums*, lavenders, roses, and sage add color and scent, acting as a vibrant backdrop to the extension while also adding interest. Low-level ferns and woodland plants add interest to the newly formed steps and raised bed while also lightening the area from its previous overgrown state. A newly designed wood store with cedar-shingled roof and a hazel hurdle fence add to the naturalistic aesthetic, while the sculpture fence and gate add year-round interest and a sense of playful spontaneity to the space.

All existing stone was integrated into the design and reused with wall stone and copings sourced from a local stone yard. American yellow pine was used for all timber work, offering the most sustainable alternative to tropical hardwoods or treated softwoods.

Queen Anne Gardens

Robert Edson Swain, Inc.

Seattle, United States
13,150 square feet (1222 square meters)

Photography / Ken Gutmaker, Andrew Ryznar

This project involved the landscaping to complement a renovation and extension of a heritage residence—designed by Arthur Loveless—to create a new 2800-square-foot (260-square-meter) guest house.

With a summer pavilion that was more of a sculptural landscape element than a building, the design maximized views of Puget Sound to the southwest while minimizing impact to the site and neighbors' views. Solar-passive materials extend the enjoyment of this garden retreat well into the off season.

Site plan

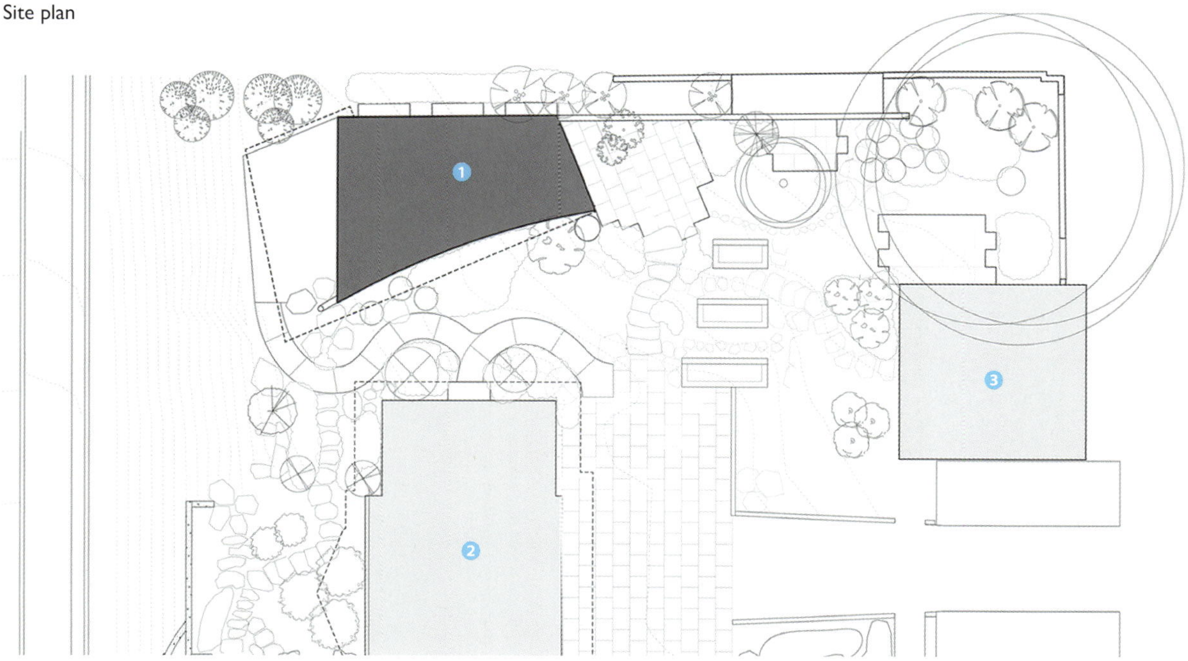

1. Pavilion
2. Existing home
3. Garage

A garden retreat in the city, wood detailed with metals and functional stone elements, dominate the interior and exterior. Existing materials were reused as much as possible, along with naturally weathering materials appropriated to the Pacific Northwest climate, which require little to no maintenance. Stone was creatively repurposed in the landscape.

A covered breezeway connects the two modern cabins—one of which houses the kitchen, dining area, guest quarters, entertainment cantina, and utility functions, while the other provides a more private space with a loft-like sleeping and working studio. The outdoor passage allows the spaces to stay comfortable year-round in the maritime Pacific Northwest climate.

Part of the peace found on the property is the result of determination to utilize plants generally considered native to the region. Once established, these plants generally require lower levels of maintenance and resources than exotic options. The landscape supports and is supported by existing environmental conditions.

Saratoga hillside estate

Design Focus International

Saratoga, United States
43,560 square feet (4046 square meters)

Photography / Lauren Devon

The design challenge for this project was to create an estate garden on a steep landslide site with an existing retaining wall. Design Focus International took on the challenge, creating a series of beautiful outdoor rooms at different levels. Since the project was on a landslide site, the design had to allow for reconstruction in the event of more slippage. Because of this, the design team selected imported antique walkway stones from London that were 4 inches (10 centimeters) thick—requiring no mortar or concrete to install—and used dry stone walls for the retaining walls. Both of these could be put back together if the hill ever slipped again. Happily, all aspects have stayed in place.

The design team raised the grade of the pool area by 3 feet (90 centimeters) to better connect the upper level kitchen and family room with the entertaining area and removed a low garage window to create a backdrop for the fireplace and entertaining area. Because the pool could only be 28 feet (8.5 meters) long due to landslide restrictions, the design team sought to make it look like a jewel and incorporated glass tile on the bottom and along the waterline in shades of copper and green. They also added bronze water sprays from the edges of the pool.

The terraced stone stairs and raised beds create a beautiful and dramatic view from the house while increasing usability on the steep site. At the bottom of the stairs the team designed a formal flower garden that could be changed with the seasons to create interest and provide a focal point. A sweeping meadow offered access to the pool terrace via Sally Holmes roses and lavender.

The bocce ball court and fire-pit area were placed at the top of the site to provide another destination with a commanding view. The scope of work included design and site supervision for all elements including master planning, grading, drainage, planting, irrigation, lighting, and masonry.

1. Terrace
2. Meadow
3. Sculpture
4. Pond
5. Lawn
6. Proposed arbor
7. Cobble drainage swail
8. Meadow path
9. Dry stone retaining walls
10. Residence

Hardscape plan

Cluny House

Guz Architects

The Cluny House was designed around a central water court that forms the focal point of the project. Lushly planted roof gardens surround this and add to the effect that nature is evident in every part of the house.

On this relatively small site at the end of a cul-de-sac, the designers created this tropical courtyard house with two pavilions on an L-shaped plan overlooking a water garden comprising a large fishpond with an archipelago of tree-filled islands, which appears to merge with a lap pool encased in a sheer glass rim.

Singapore

12,540 square feet (1165 square meters)

Photography / Patrick Bingham Hall

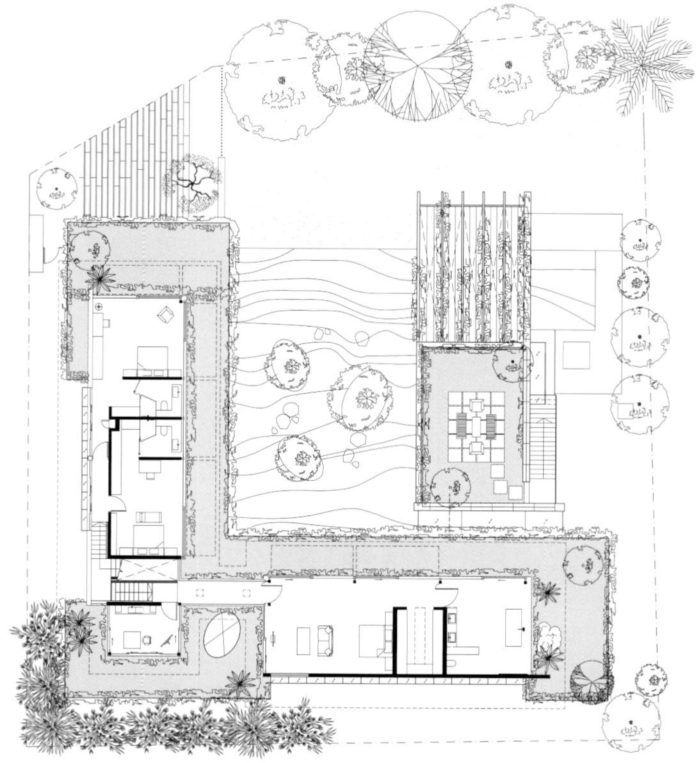

Second-floor plan

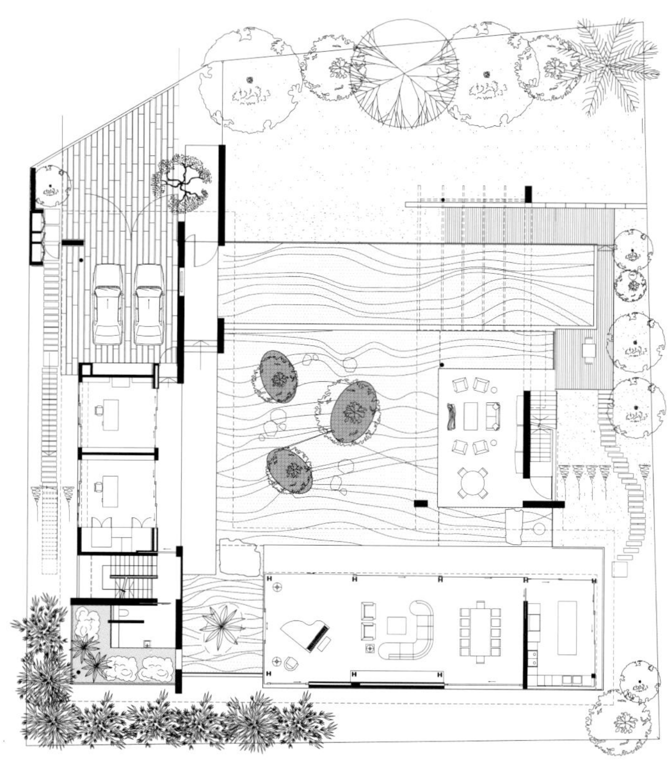

First-floor plan

The Cluny House reinforces the oft-repeated observation that small tropical houses come alive when water is used as the focal point of a central courtyard. The scale and transparency of the landscape and the reflections of the sky and trees in the pond conspire to amplify the space, while the water garden also works to draw the eye away from the architectural structure of the house itself. By cantilevering second floor roof gardens along the length of the uniform elevation, the designers created a barrier of greenery to screen the upper level, so that the mass of the house appears recessed, hidden by the plantings. Further visual trickery was employed in the landscaping to hide the proportions of the architecture. The concern was that the proportions of the open veranda, projecting into the water garden, would appear short and stubby, so a vine-draped trellis was constructed over the pool to continue the form and length of the veranda.

The Cluny House was orientated towards its views, but every view is internal, confined within the boundaries of the site. The designers created a completely self-referential world, which provides its own delights and offers its own micro-climate. The most sublime vista is to be had from the long L-shaped walkway beneath the lip of the cantilevered roof gardens, where the low wide soffits ripple and sparkle in the sunlight reflected from the surface of the ponds.

Photovoltaic cells and solar water heaters were employed together with the design for passive cooling and cross-ventilation to reduce energy usage. Irrigation tanks and roof gardens collect and recycle rainwater; and the use of materials such as recycled teak and artificial timber adds warmth without compromising finite environmental resources. This integration of technology and nature deserves special mention in this compelling design that, which realistically become the model for sustainable living.

Villa garden Hendrik-Ido-Ambacht

Erik van Gelder

Hendrik-Ido-Ambacht, The Netherlands
2133 square feet (650 square meters)

Photography / Peter Baas

Erik van Gelder designed a garden that perfectly matches the detached house, built in a contemporary country style. The plot is comfortable and intimate, as well as attractive and pragmatic. The designer took into account the couple's functional demands—without compromising on style.

The Corten steel material, which was used on the window panels, was liberally repeated throughout the garden—from fencing for privacy and shelter to panels that run over the floor right into the garden partition. The rusty metal makes a strong architectural statement. Its rich and earthy tones compliment the evergreen trees, which visually break the long continuous lines. They were cleverly planted to be viewed from inside the house.

The residents enjoy tranquility and stunning views from the porch at the back of the house. Partitions in wood, stone, and weathering steel at strategic locations lead the eye and create a sense of intimacy. The natural-stone wall defines the contemporary pond, with water pouring smoothly from stainless-steel tubes. A wooden fence centrally located in the back of the garden demarcates the lawn, which is the children's play area. Massive polyester planters were filled with low-growing ornamental grasses and little trees—a pleasing design contrast with the shiny white pots.

The lounge area in the back of the garden contains a wooden deck for lazing out in the sun, a whirlpool, and a sauna—the perfect anti-stress program! Erik integrated some smart design features, including invisible outdoor speakers for perfect sound, a "window with a view" in the sauna, and LED-lighting for an enchanting atmosphere.

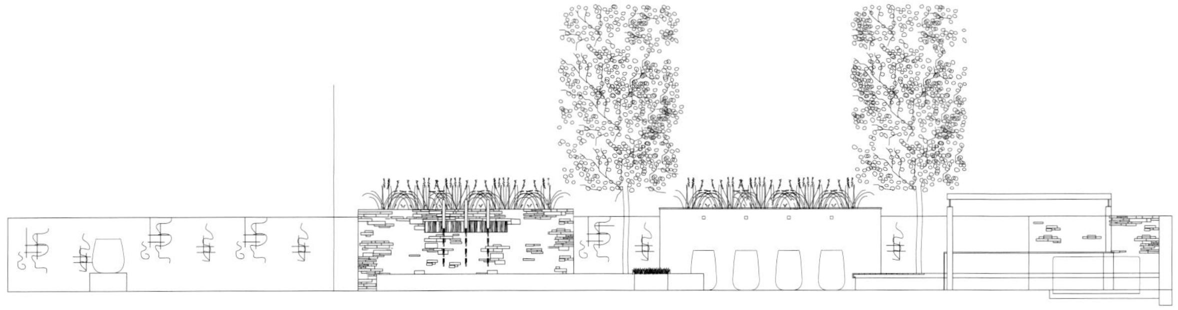

Elevation

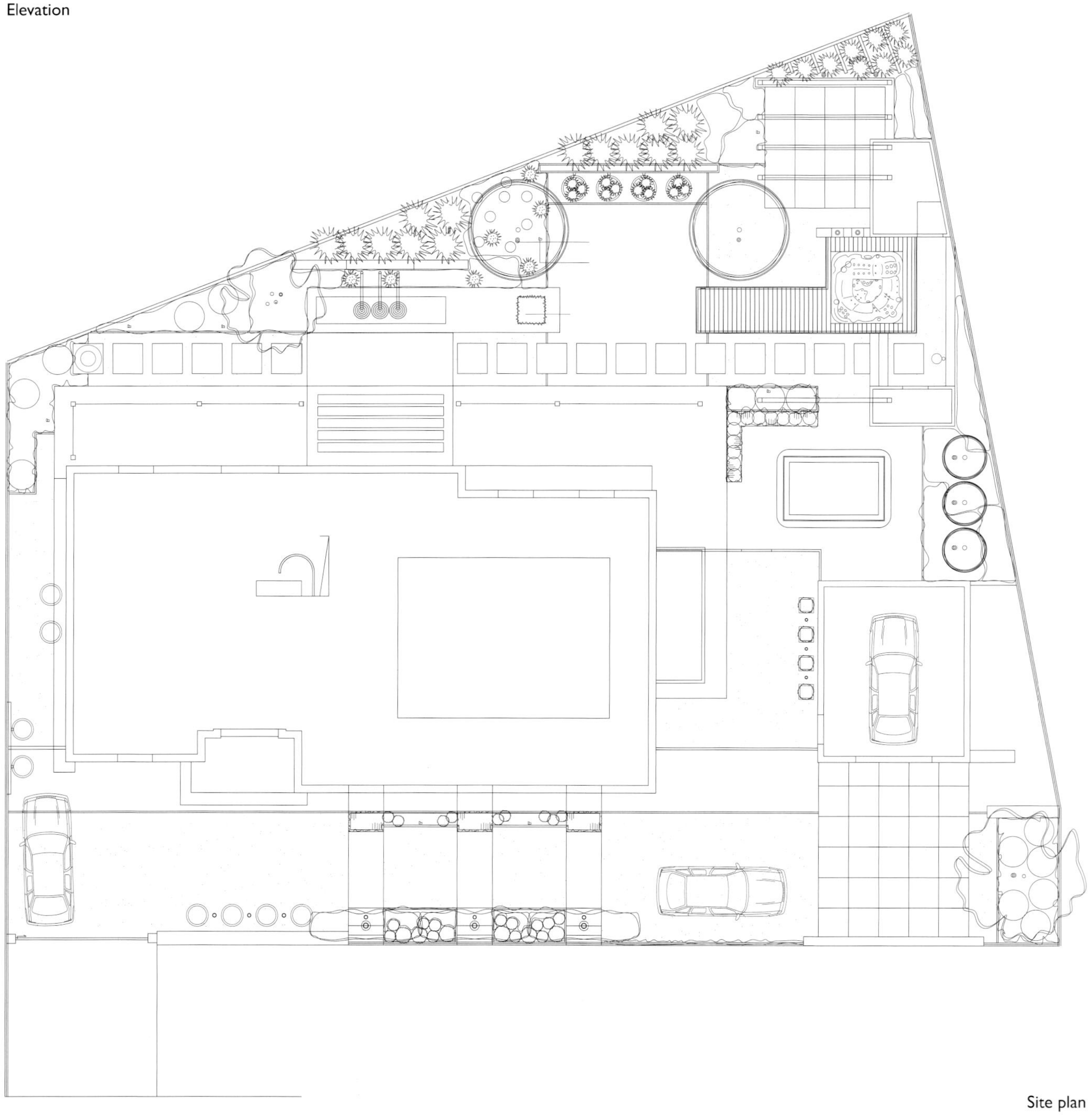

Site plan

The Touraine Garden

R. Youngblood & Co.

This residential estate in Oakland County, Michigan offers a timeless and classical feel within both the architecture and the gardens. Within the sprawling private acres are several gardens and outdoor spaces, each of which provide a unique experience.

The main entry includes matching large-scale boxwood parterres. A traditional design to the front brick walls, bluestone walks and custom limestone provide the ambience of a classic French garden. Custom gas lanterns with flickering flames were positioned throughout to lend the feel of a timeless estate. Sitting adjacent to the boxwoods are companion plants such as Annabelle hydrangea and lavender.

The estate is entered via an old-world driveway of authentic granite Belgium block, each piece of which was individually set with its random size and thickness. At the center of the motor court is a traditional medallion of smooth granite tiles of 24 x 24 inches (61 x 61 centimeters).

Adjacent to the motor court sits the entry to the "secret garden." Tall brick walls frame the perimeter and allow for the anchoring of a custom wrought-iron gate, which was built by a local metal artist. At the center of the arch of the iron gate hangs a copper gas lantern and at the heart of the secret garden, a bronze cherub is gracefully layered by seasonal color displays of selected flowers. Oft backdropped by calming classical music from the house, the garden is softly lit at night by two custom-built gas wall sconces.

Oakland County, Michigan, United States

88,000 square feet (8200 square meters)

Photography / Joe Vaughn

The lower patio space provides a much more casual experience with the use of large natural limestone walls. A relaxed plant pallet of river birch, boxwood (*Pachysandra*) and woodland ferns softens the space. Moss covered bluestone and an understory shade dominated environment make it the perfect place to cool and relax on hot summer days.

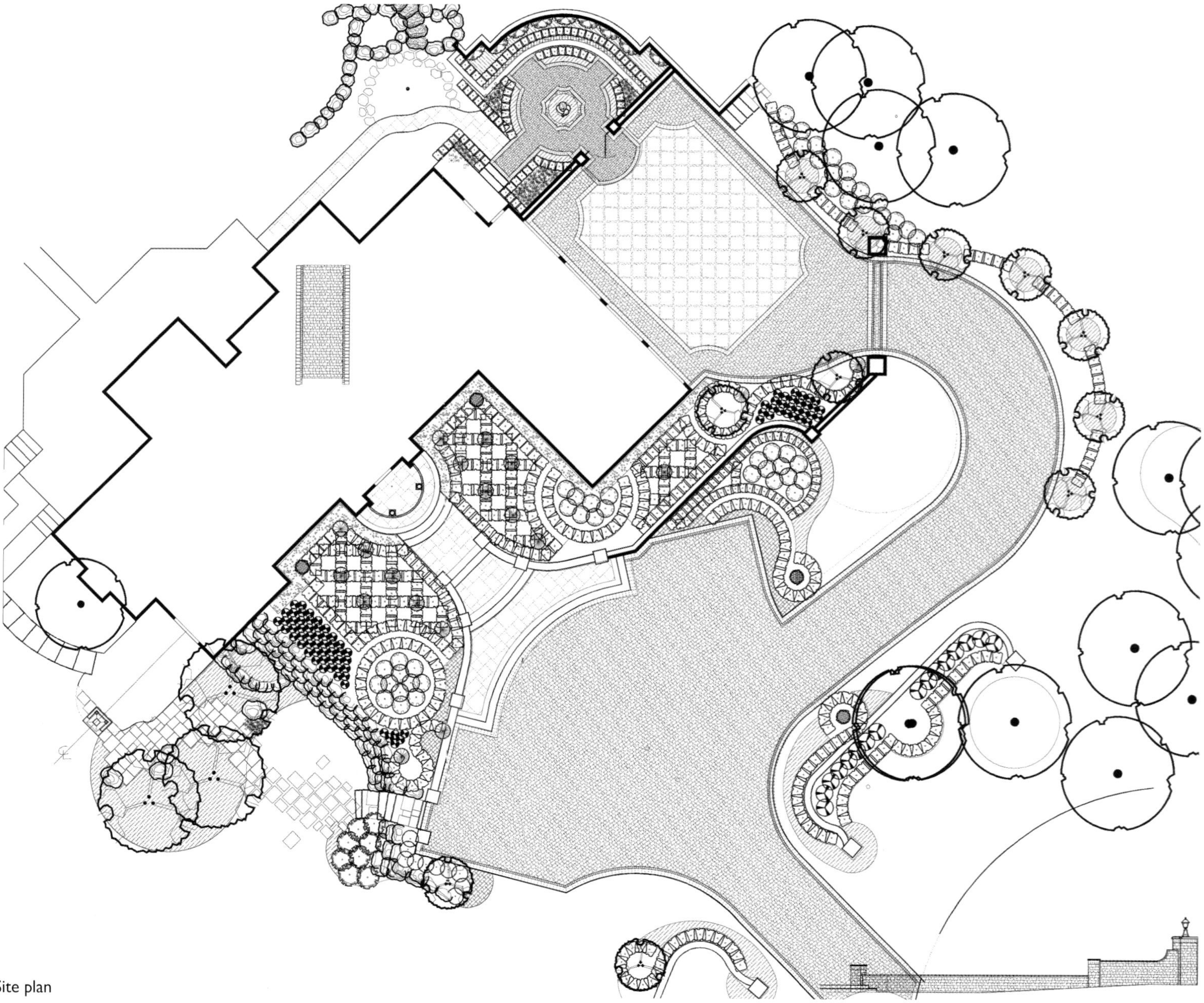

Site plan

Ditton Rd traditional garden

Lynne Marcus Garden and Landscape Design

Surrey, United Kingdom
3617 square feet (336 square meters)

Photography / Jacek Wac, Matthew Gilbert

A busy professional couple required a classic yet semi-traditional garden to complement their Victorian villa and the shabby chic internal décor. The garden was to be enjoyed for relaxation, entertaining, and as an ever-changing backdrop to the conservatory that they used throughout the year. The brief included a dining area, water, a summerhouse, hedging, lollipops, neighbor screening, and a richly colored plant palette.

Linear geometry anchors the landscape with the house. The main axis was centered on the conservatory and a pond, raised to be visible from inside the house, which strengthens the central axis to draw the eye to the length of the garden across a runner and carpet of lawn. A secondary axis was centered to the side with lounge access, guiding the eye down the path and the long view through the garden to the summerhouse. Staggered, offset symmetry gave pace, balance, and a fresh, contemporary twist to traditional symmetrical formality.

Raised planting beds by the house bridged the level change between the house and the raised pond. Random-laid, sawn York stone, tumbled setts, and crunchy aggregate gives a modern, uncluttered finish to the traditional materials and layout. Hedging, topiary, ornamental trees, ferns, and grasses provide an evergreen framework for rich oranges and purples, giving way to distant whites and cornflower blue to pick up the color of the summerhouse.

A line of mountain-ash (*Sorbus aucuparia*) was used to screen neighboring houses. Wire work benches were set for planting, reading, or quiet reflection. Large lead planters and occasional pots and urns add character and interest.

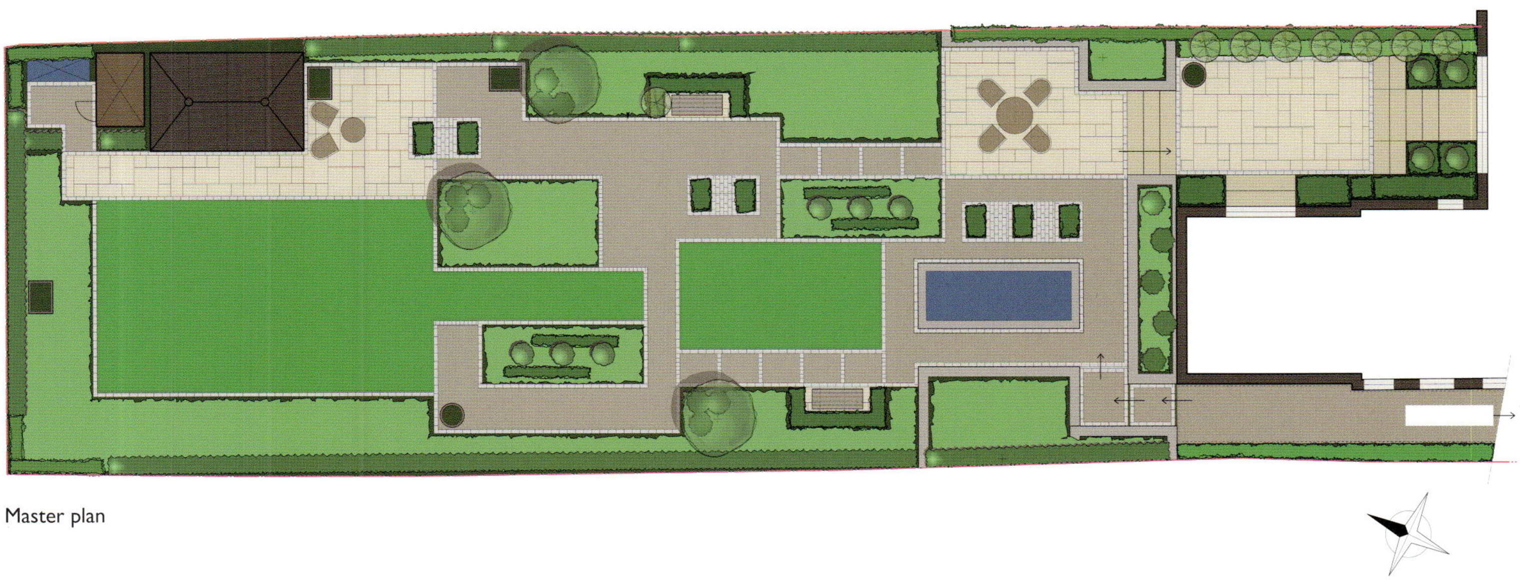

Master plan

Bridle Path Estate 2

Janet Rosenberg & Studio, Giancarlo Garofalo Architect Inc.

Toronto, Canada

7536 square feet (700 square meters)

Photography / Jeff McNeill Photography

Color and texture abound in the extensive renovation of the Bridle Path garden. Janet Rosenberg & Studio was invited by the architect, Giancarlo Garofalo, to prepare a master plan for a complete garden renovation that would be integrated with an entirely new rear façade of the residence.

The new architectural footprint was marked by a distribution of structures that illustrate an incremental geometric growth pattern, which in its totality attains a sheltering enclosure of private outdoor space. By way of this distributed layout, the architecture not only harbors the active landscape of the pool environment, but most importantly plays part of a diversified vocabulary in stone, with hard and soft elements of the landscape necessarily inlayed and inserted within the architectural fabric of materials and forms.

In particular, the pool terrace is unmistakably a genuine expression of the site, and it is where the wide range of Zen-inspired taste for colorful and textured plantings is harbored. It is also here that the multiple planes of the terraces create a visual and functional interplay with the landscape, as interlaced areas that respond to each other, much like the highly diverse liminal nature of a river landscape, which fluctuates between wet and dry.

1 Sod
2 Existing residence
3 Deck
4 Pool

Rear yard plan

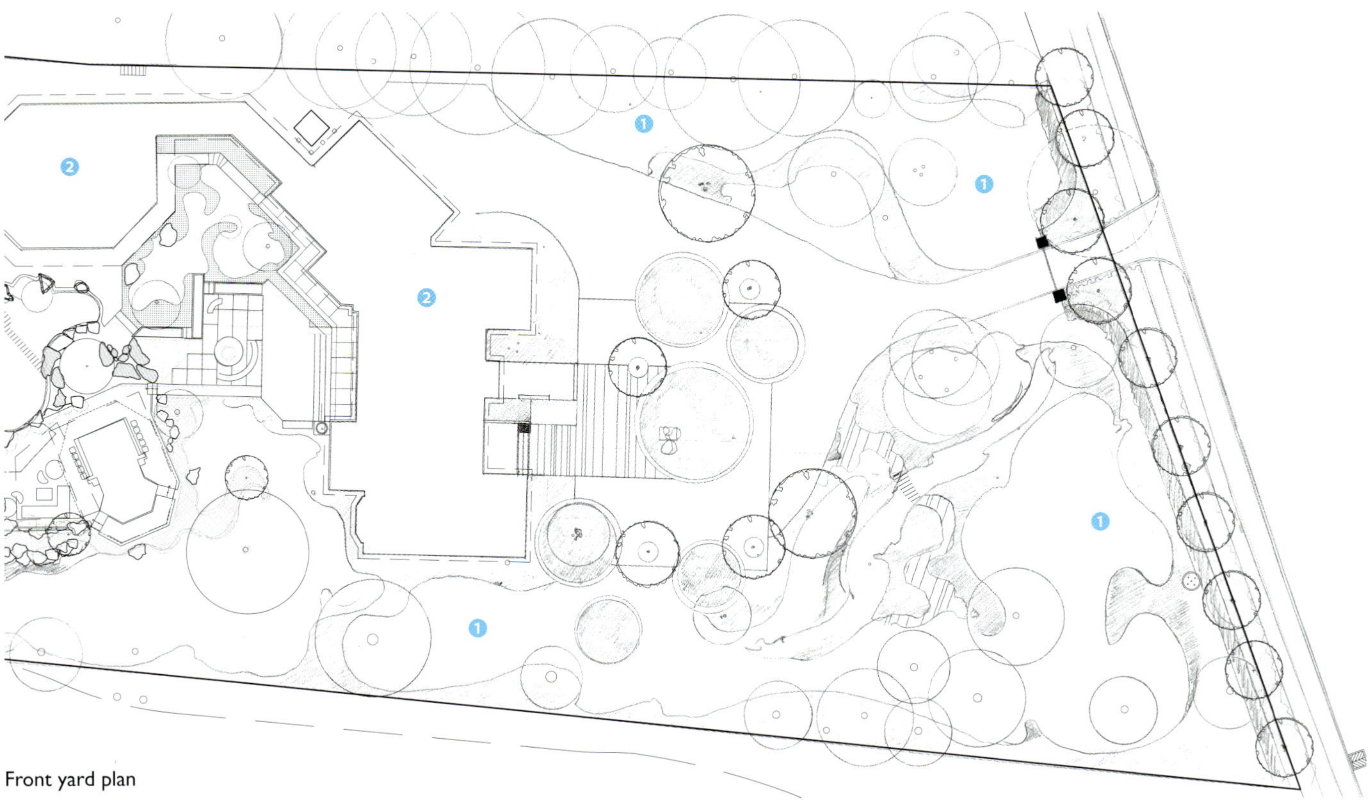

Front yard plan

At the same time, the circular form—clearly evident in the landscape plan—thematically links the front entry court with the pool terrace, on the one hand echoing the canopy of specimen trees, while also creating circular garden islands of intensive diversity, creating zones of focus within the greater woodland site.

The entry to the residence is defined by a slight stair ascent to the ground floor and is marked by the sight and sound of water in this transition between outside and inside. Satisfying an increasingly important contemporary goal, the design certainly accommodates modern living's aspirations for extending the architecture into the landscape, along with the comforts of the interiors.

In the details, the texture of the rocks further expands the range of textures in terms of porosity, echoed as well in the contrast between stepping stones and the apparent liquidity of the driving surface. All boulders were hand selected from the quarry in Wharton, Ontario. The materiality of stone was further expressed through varied forms and finishes, both sleek and rugged Eramousa stone of the Owen Sound area, enriching in its choreography the multi-faceted characteristics of the garden.

Family garden at Kenwood, Hampstead

Lynne Marcus Garden and Landscape Design, Charlton Brown

London, United Kingdom
16,146 square feet (1500 square meters)

Photography / Jacek Wac, Matthew Gilbert, Tony Murray

A new, multi-level garden was required to complement a house renovation for a family with two young boys and their African tortoise. The brief was to create an elegant, semi-traditional, symmetrical garden, with direct access via a lower ground courtyard to an indoor swimming pool in the basement of the house. They also required a loggia with a kitchen for outside leisure and entertaining, a vivarium for the tortoise, a large lawn for football, and a planting palette restricted to mostly green and white.

Both linear and curvilinear geometry anchors the house to the landscape. Sawn scoutmoor stone reflects shades of gray to tie the interior with the landscape. A central axis of symmetry extends from the front door of the house to the rear of the garden and a secondary axis was centered on the family room to the loggia. The lower pool courtyard offers space for seating around a fire table. A lead-clad water cistern and palms and ferns add an exotic touch and form a composed view from the pool and upper floors.

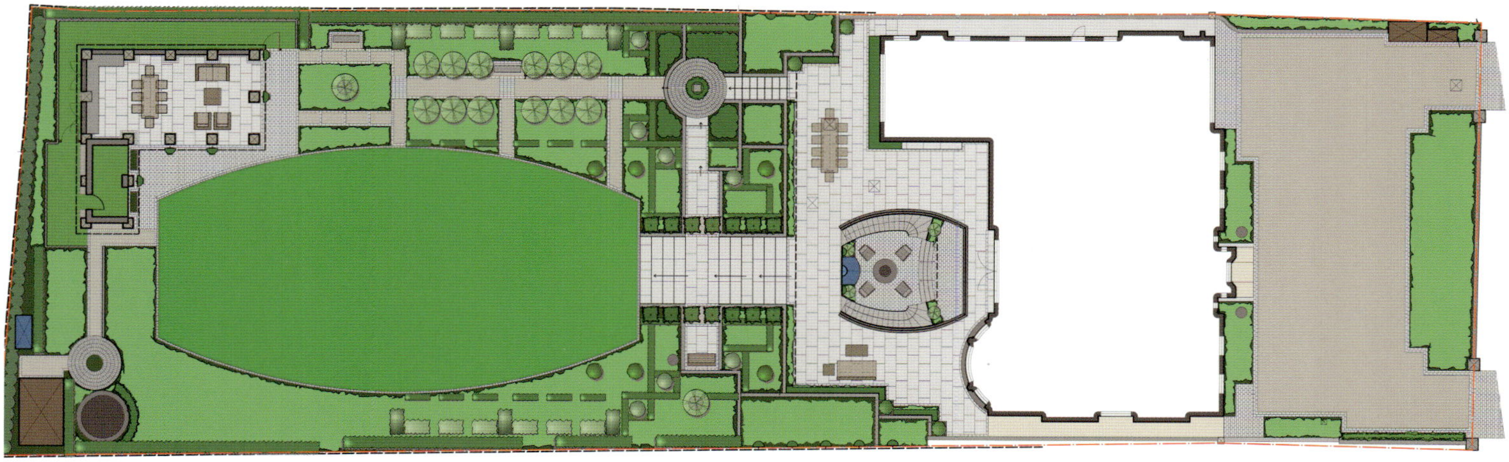

Master plan

A symmetrical pair of Italianate-style staircases—with railings that echo the internal staircase—lead up from the courtyard to link with the main terrace, integrating the courtyard with the garden and central view. The garden incline is terraced and planted as a contemporary, three-dimensional box parterre filled with small, white roses and soft under-planting.

Graceful steps flanked with evergreen oak (*Quercus ilex*) lead to the elliptical lawn and to a pathway through an arching "Cornus avenue" to the loggia (designed by the architect) to the rear. Hedging, domes, cubes, and pillars strengthen the architecture of the garden but give way to more organic planting to the rear. Ornamental trees, billowing hedges of hydrangea, and fresh, seasonal planting of roses, herbaceous plants, grasses, ferns, and bulbs deliver constant, seasonal change.

French-inspired private garden

Design Focus International, Rebecca Dye principal

San Jose, California, United States
43,560 square feet (4047 square meters)

Photography / Lauren Devon

The client asked Design Focus International to design a white garden with French influences that would relate to the architecture of the original 1920s home. The garden entry was crafted with detailed brick walls and iron gates, which lead visitors to the antique granite entry path and courtyard. The granite stones were several hundred years old and imported from China. A large pond filled with white water lilies and shimmering gold fish served as the centerpiece of the courtyard. For the center of the pond, the designers found a large antique urn and filled it with seasonal flowers.

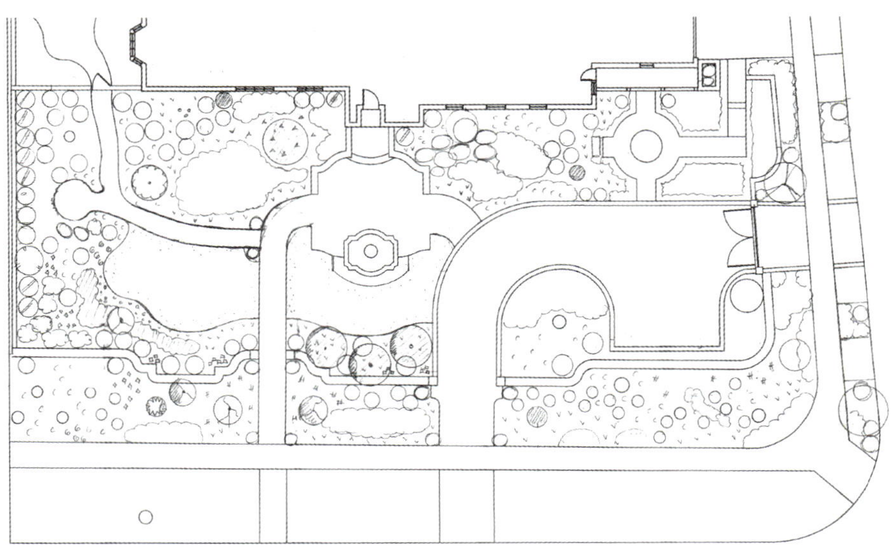

Planting plan

Walking past a classic French iron gazebo, the path leads to the library garden—a quiet space for relaxation and reflection. For this area, the designers included several pieces of antique sculpture as well as a French limestone wall fountain.

The main bluestone terrace was designed to serve large groups while still being in scale with the home and creating a sense of intimacy through elements such as the spectacular outdoor fireplace, antique urns, and sculptures. The central sycamore adds intimacy by dividing up spaces for different seating areas. Iceberg roses and lavender surround the main terrace, and Sally Holmes roses climb 25 feet (7.6 meters) up the walls, giving an old-world feel to the space.

In addition to the roses, lavender, and other more formal plants, the designers incorporated a variety of plants to encourage habitat. Since completion of the project, there have been many nesting birds on the site and the owner has connected with the nature in her garden.

The Garden of Esther

Art & Jardins Conception

Mont-Saint-Hilaire, Quebec, Canada
10,764 square feet (1000 square meters)

Photography / Jean-Claude Hurni

Given a carte blanche by the owners not subject to any constraint or requirement whatsoever, Art & Gardens Design were able to design a landscape that reflected the owners' personality and feelings. Furthermore, the designers sought to create an exterior design that was directly related to the interior of the residence.

As inviting as the people who live there, the façade of the beautiful house reveals side paths that lead to the back of the home where most of the garden is located. The existing landscape had a good elevation of ground, along with an inground pool and a stone wall, which had to be taken into consideration to ensure the old elements wedded well with the new materials and equipment. In order to create a garden environment that would be frequented daily and inhabitable both day and night, it was necessary to ensure that everything was well integrated and harmonious.

The result was a pleasant outdoor living environment that exceeded the expectations of both the owners and designers providing an inviting space to enjoy privately or with guests.

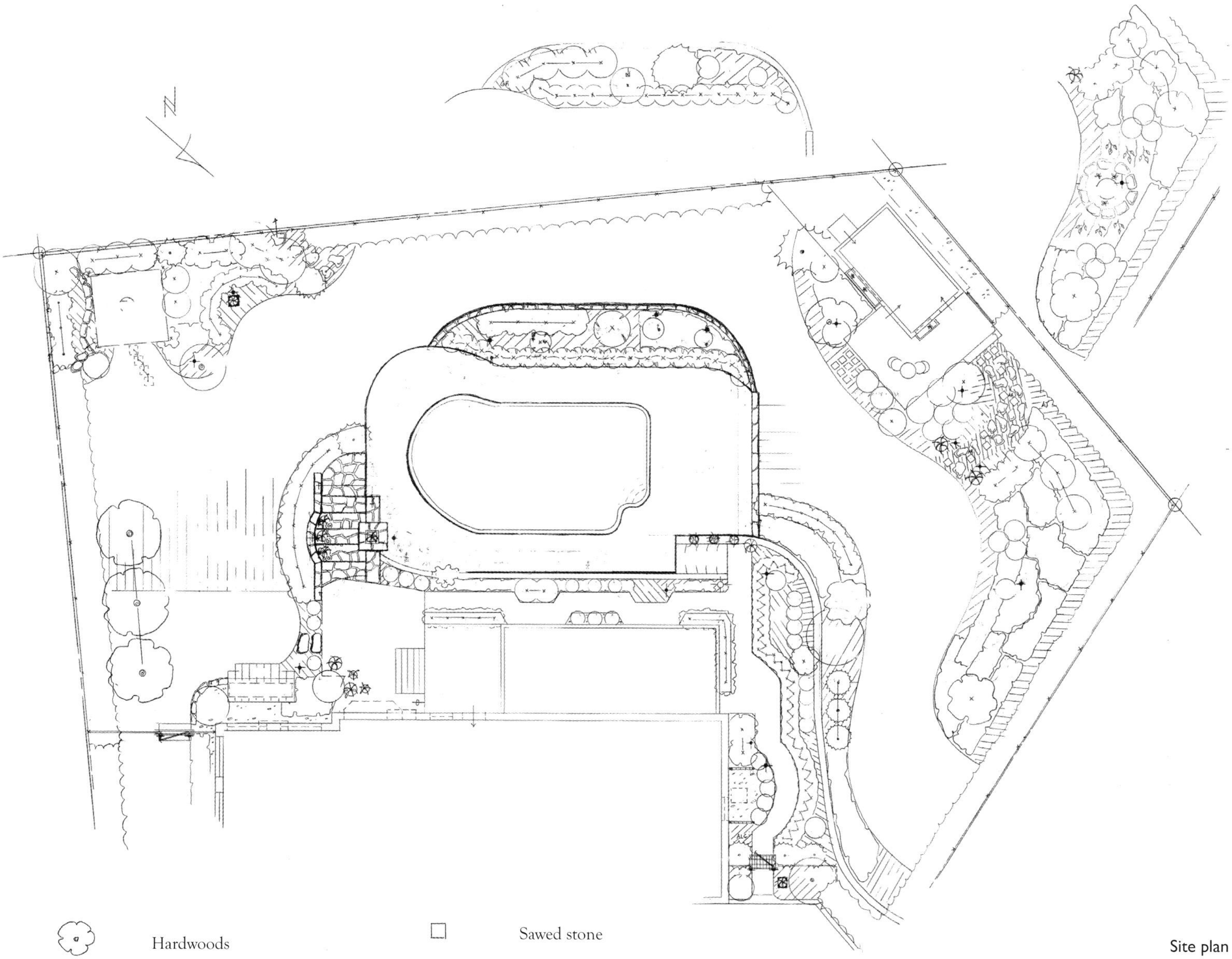

Hardwoods
Hardwood shrubs
Conifers
Perennials
Flower urn
Stone wall
Silica stone or bluestone
Sawed stone
Pebble
Door and window
Fence
Tap
Lamp

Site plan

466

Kirkwood House

Jailmake Ltd

The Kirkwood garden was designed to work as a low-maintenance kitchen garden that reconnects the 1960s terrace house with the outdoors. The overall layout was designed to make it both easy to work in and easy to entertain in.

The crisscross path is wide enough to push a wheelbarrow through and leads to both a potting shed area and a chicken coup at the bottom of the garden, which are sheltered from the worst of the rain by the overhanging branches of an old Conifer. In the center of the garden, an in-built fire pit is not only useful for burning garden waste but also transforms this central area of the garden into an inviting space for socializing in summer evenings.

London, United Kingdom
538 square feet (50 square meters)

Photography / Rory Gardiner, Ollie Hammick

The wooden fences behind the planters were painted black to make them fade into the background, while the warm earthy tones of the Corten steel planters beautifully compliment the greens of the foliage and the blue-gray of the slate gravel. The planters were designed to stand 3.3 feet (1 meter) tall, making the garden easy to maintain without kneeling or bending. The height of the beds also means that the garden benefits from being planted with trailing plants, like the parrot beak (*Lotus berthelotii*) with its silvery-green foliage that shines out against the orange tones of the steel.

1 Deck
2 Herbs
3 Pond
4 Vegetables
5 Chickens

Sketch

The layout of the planters make good use of the available space with two of the eight beds reserved for growing produce. The central bed nearest to the house is used for herbs and salad leaves alone, whilst the other central bed at the rear of the garden is for seasonal vegetables, with the south-facing aspect of the garden making it ideal for growing tomatoes in the summer. These two planters were designed so that one can walk 360 degrees around them both, making them easier to plant, weed, and maintain throughout the year.

Simple movable perches, made from ash and steel were designed to be suspended from the edge of the planters and can be moved with you around the garden to be either perched in the sun or to use for resting gardening tools and coffee whilst while working.

At the center of either side of the garden are two lower beds. A young fig tree enjoys the warmth and sunshine of the southeast facing aspect during the summer and sits nestled among a mixture of *Crocus* (iris), daffodils and *Fritillaria* (lily) in the spring, while the soothing sound of gently trickling water comes from the goldfish pond that sits opposite. The beds on either side of the pond are home to a variety of plants including various grasses, ferns, and bamboo, which add both textural interest year round and various evergreen shades throughout the winter months.

Bi-fold doors open out onto a section of decking, which not only provides ample space for a small table and chairs for breakfasts outside, but also houses a variety of potted plants. Slightly sheltered by the house, this space works as a nursery for young seedlings in the spring and provides plenty of fresh air for potted succulents to enjoy in the summer months. The deck was designed so that it runs flush with the floor level inside the house, making it easy to take the main dining table and chairs outside for entertaining on warm summer nights.

The Lakeshore Garden

R. Youngblood & Co.

Goodrich, Michigan, United States
58,885 square feet (5471 square meters)

Photography / Jeff Garland

As this large residential site was situated on a steep hillside at the lake's edge, the location required large-scale stone retainage in order to allow the site to be buildable. As such, 600 tons of Canadian limestone was used to build retaining walls and stone steps. The large stone walls took four month to construct and the overall project took 12 months to complete.

Incorporated among the stone, several gathering areas and patios were created to enjoy the views of the lake. Plantings were designed to soften the stone and add color to the environment. Within the overall property, one can select different areas to sit and enjoy the lake views, all of which offer a different experience.

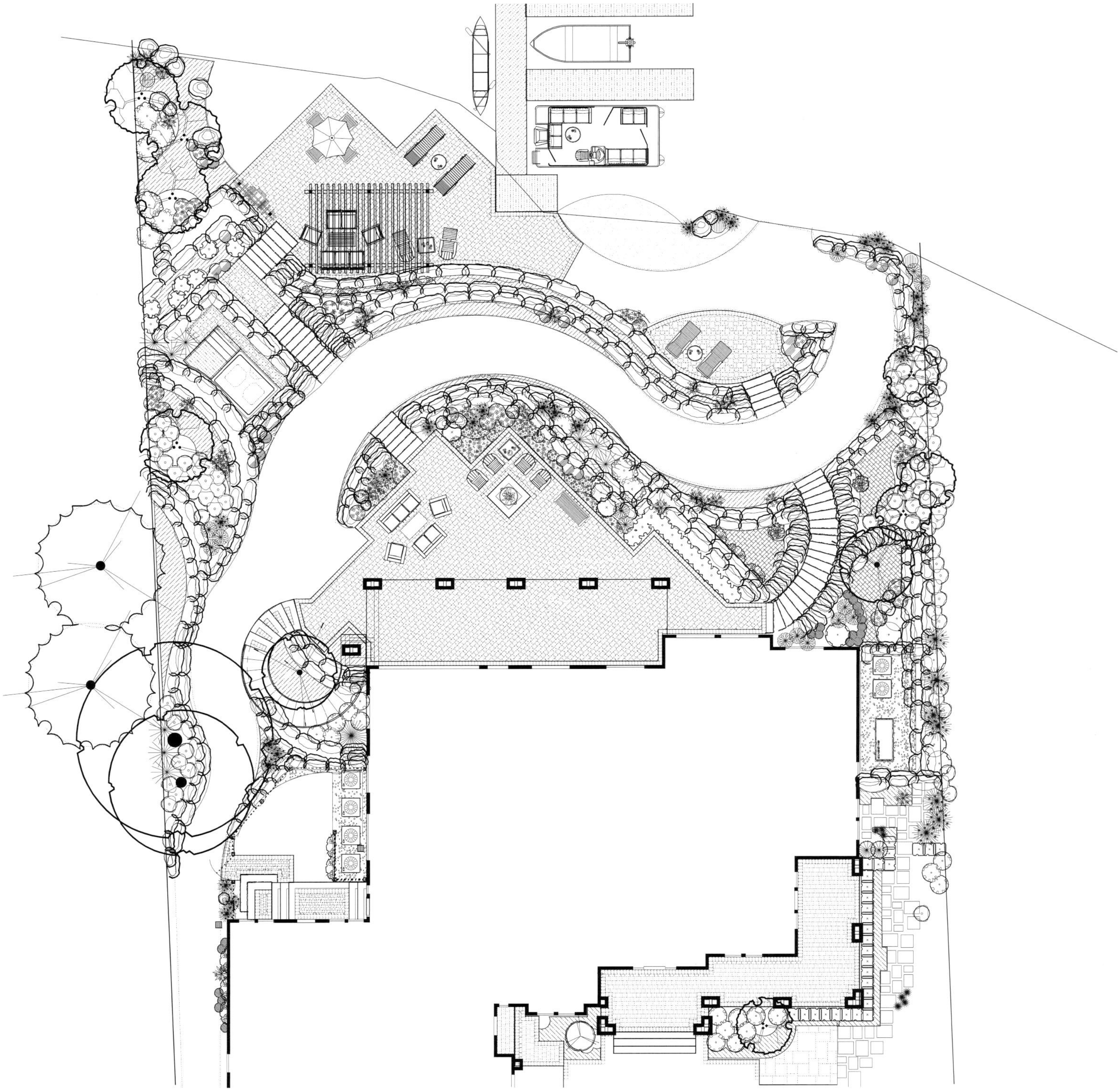

Site plan

The upper patio provides the most elevated views and includes a large wood-burning fire pit to keep everyone warm as the days cool. A spa is situated among the stone walls mid-way down providing a smaller, more intimate experience. At the lake level, a large patio shaded by a custom-built cedar pergola allows a true lakefront experience and provides access to the boats and lake. In the evenings, the space becomes softly illuminated with the strategically designed landscape lighting.

Phinney residence

Robert Edson Swain, Inc.

Seattle, United States
4500 square feet (418 square meters)

Photography / Clive Nichols, Ken Gutmaker, Robert Edson Swain, Inc.

Within this year-round retreat located 10 minutes from downtown Seattle in the United States, the dense and abundant landscape of native evergreen and deciduous plantings provides delightful solitude from the nearby city center.

One-hundred-and-sixty-eight native plant species were carefully placed to edit neighbor views and seclude the home from the city, while still offering views of Seattle, Puget Sound, and the Olympic Mountains. Subtle and diverse, the plantings provide peace and unexpected discoveries, while these native—once established—require lower levels of water, maintenance, and resources than exotic options, and offer a lush, sequential sense of seasonal change.

The home is protected from the street by mountain hemlocks (*Tsuga mertensiana*). Upon entering, one walks along cedar planks, passing below the canopy of a Douglas fir (*Pseudotsuga menziesii*), vine maples (*Acer circinatum*), and quaking aspen (*Populous tremuloides*), which all provide elegance, lushness, and shelter. A copper spigot, Chinese granite well marker, and large basalt basin form a water feature, sheltering street noise.

Landscape and architecture are one in this setting. The exterior of the home uses rusted steel detailing, western redcedar beams, and cedar shingle siding to blend with the natural character of the landscape. Careful and efficient space utilization and detailing is opportune and succeeds in a time when living spaces need be smaller, furthering the sense of peace and seclusion in the city.

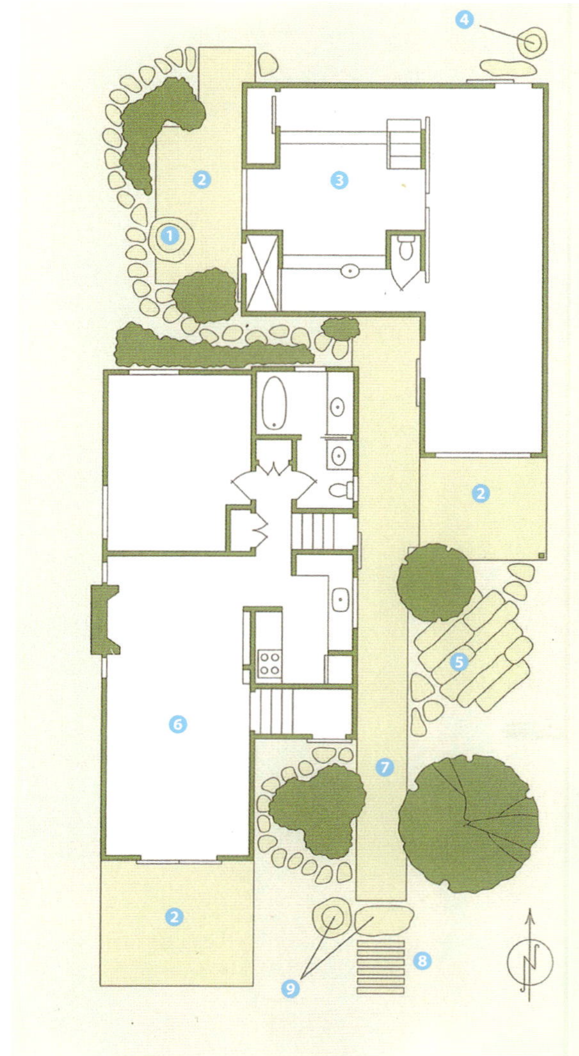

Site plan

1. Ancient Chinese stone soak hub
2. Deck
3. Back cabin
4. Stone water basin
5. Patio
6. Front cabin
7. Cedar boardwalk
8. Cedar planks
9. Granite stepping stone and Japanese water basin

Wildlife flowers such as pacific bleeding heart (*Dicentra formosa*) and western trillium bloom in the spring and sit beside sword ferns (*Polystichum munitum*) and rhododendron, softening the Chinese stone elements of the landscape. The garden includes white and pink fawn lilies (*Erythronium revolutum*), camas (*Camassia quamash*) Stika mist-maiden (*Romanzoffia sitchensis*), all were cultivated from seeds and bulbs.

A fluid story of places, setting, and small gardens all contribute to the remarkable sense of solitude in the city.

Private garden in Mont-Saint-Hilaire

Art & Jardins Conception

Located on a large plot not far from a pretty road, the beautiful Les Résidences Soleil already had a certain charm, which begged for an accompanying garden that could pair it. A bi-generational house with a variety of accommodations, it also required both well-defined parking for both inhabitants and guests.

With a first glance from the path leading to the main entrance of the house, the designers wanted to emphasize the perspective and strengthen this line of vision with two elements: plants and an installation of a flowered urn to serve as focal point. Plantations of two small Rose Glow (*Berberis thunbergii*) hedges, Bloody Crane's-bill (*Geranium sanguineum*), and grandiflora (*Hydrangea paniculate*) served to give the appearance of a large garden to the landscaping of the frontage to somewhat soften the path.

Mont-Saint-Hilaire, Quebec, Canada
26,910 square feet (2500 square meters)

Photography / Jean-Claude Hurni

For the rest, the designers created open living areas providing a certain amount of privacy, while still being open to each other. On the far side of the house and a large section of the backyard, open rest areas with benches and stone pavements are complemented by various plants and flowers. Beyond the arbor, the well-framed backyard provides a playground for young children with sandbox and modules.

The result is a beautiful large garden that is both functional and majestic to allow generations to live together in harmony.

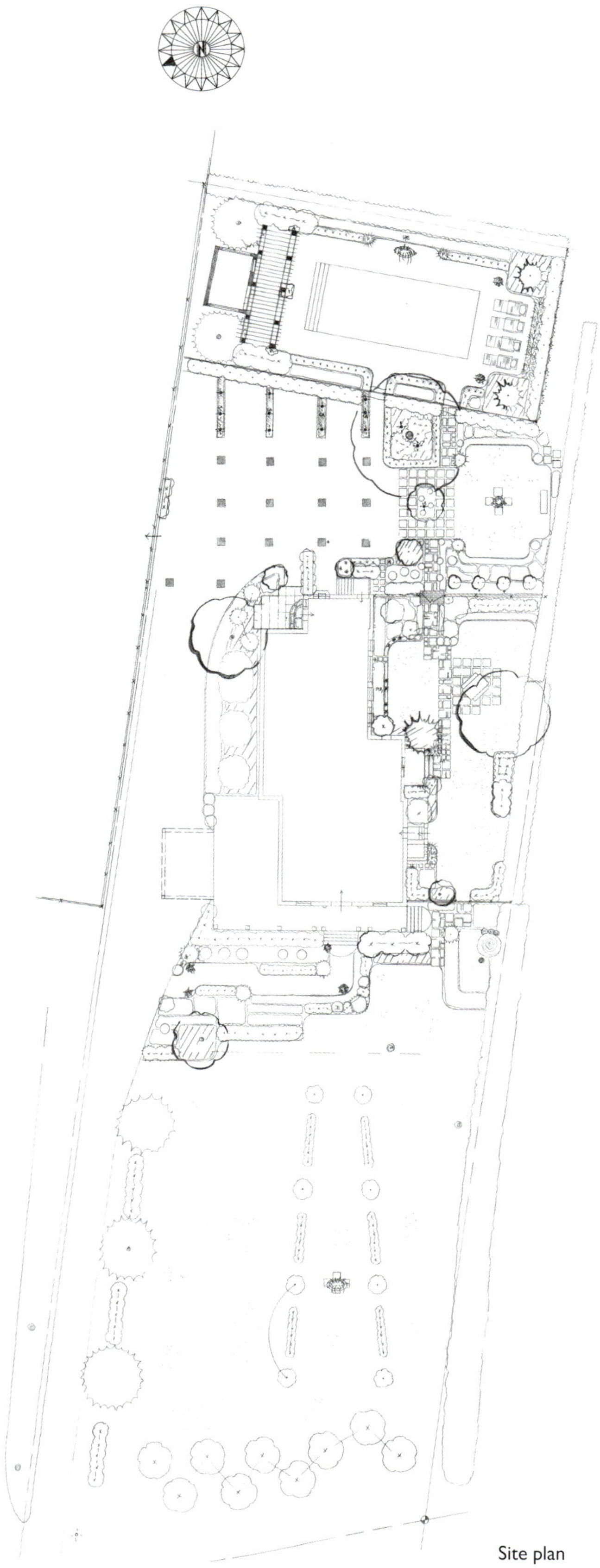

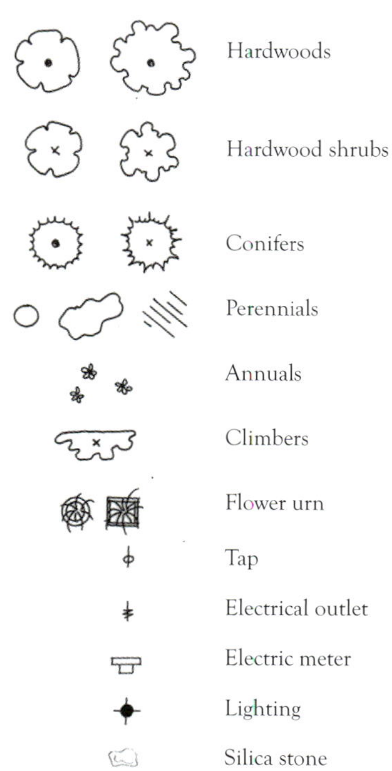
Hardwoods
Hardwood shrubs
Conifers
Perennials
Annuals
Climbers
Flower urn
Tap
Electrical outlet
Electric meter
Lighting
Silica stone

Site plan

Rattan House

Guz Architects

Located in Singapore, this dream home constructed of open-air rooms required landscaping to reflect the luxury and style in an environment that allows the internal living spaces to breathe. Comprising several rooms and their own gardens, which both protect the inhabitants and enhance privacy, the foliage works to naturally elevate the air quality and state of well-being. A contemporary interpretation of the simple and traditional courtyard house, this modern mansion was designed around a central green courtyard. The L-shaped configuration further encourages the natural ventilation and a fusion between the interior and exterior design divided only by the vegetation.

Singapore

5661 square feet (526 square meters)

Photography / Patrick Bingham Hall

First-floor plan

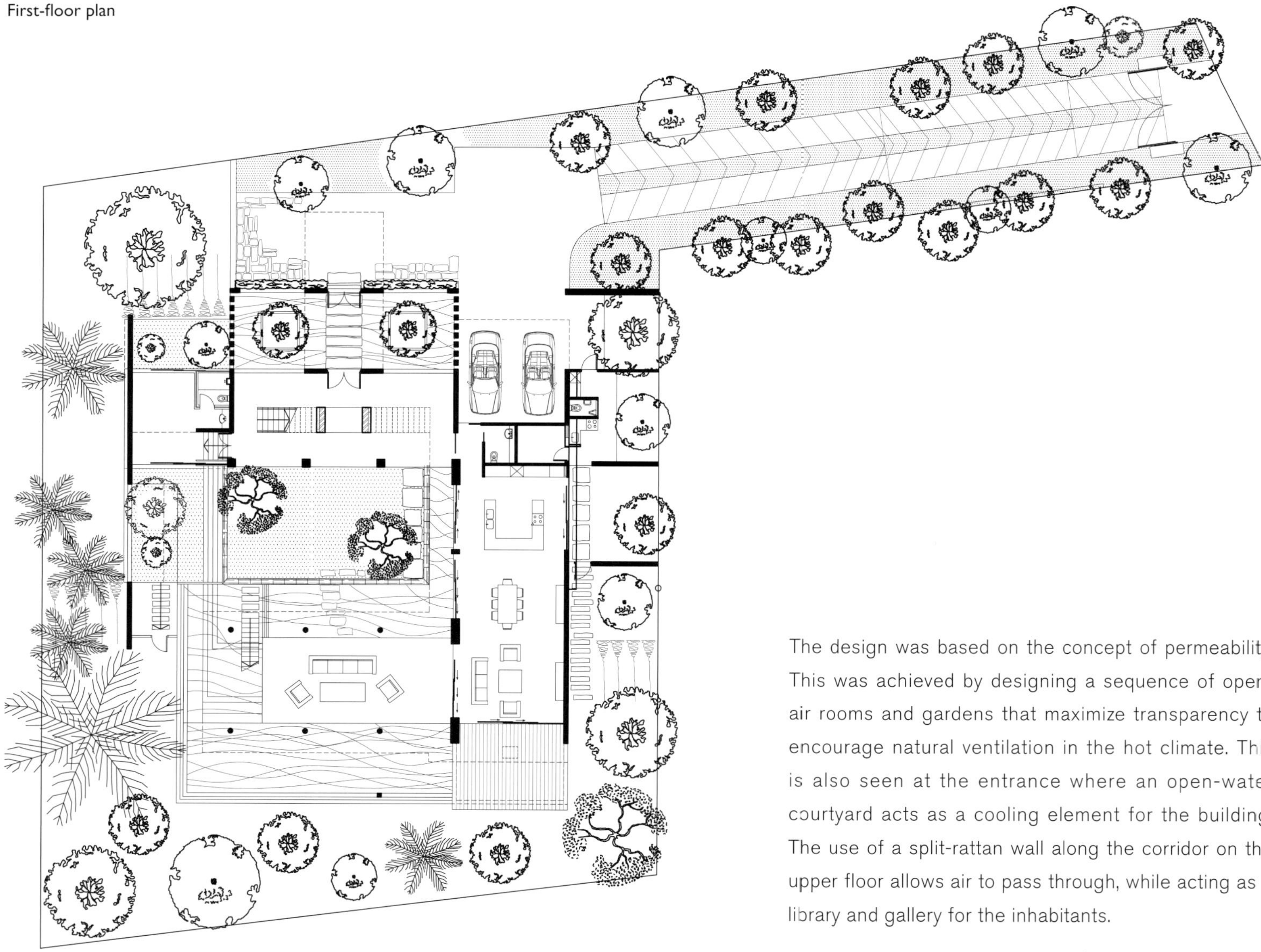

The design was based on the concept of permeability. This was achieved by designing a sequence of open-air rooms and gardens that maximize transparency to encourage natural ventilation in the hot climate. This is also seen at the entrance where an open-water courtyard acts as a cooling element for the building. The use of a split-rattan wall along the corridor on the upper floor allows air to pass through, while acting as a library and gallery for the inhabitants.

Rattan House was conceived to make the most of what is a relatively condensed site in Singapore's GCB (good class bungalow) district, with buildings all around and little breeze. The L-shaped plan was designed to make the most of the views and funnel the breezes throughout the house. Within this, the designers endeavored to create gardens and green areas to not only passively cool the house, but also to provide greenery and a sense of space that all the occupants could share.

Completed on a surprisingly low budget, rattan screens were used along the main entrance hall of the house to provide privacy, yet still allow the air to flow through.

The Chelsea Garden

R. Youngblood & Co.

Metamora, Michigan, United States
384,700 square feet (37,750 square meters)
Photography / Jeff Garland

This project was at a private residence in an area in rural Michigan known for its rolling acres and horse-farm estates with large pastures and miles of black horse board fencing following the contour of the countryside. Offering gorgeous and romantic views, the area was popular with horse lovers and equestrians.

The client's home was located high on the peak of rolling hills. The intense change in topography offered several technical challenges in both the design and the installation of the gardens, walls, and pool. Much time was spent on site to thoroughly study and understand the views to best define the location of the pool and outdoor living spaces.

Consequently, the location of the pool, the heart and soul of the project, was selected for its amazing views of the property and the large pond located at the foot of the hills. An intimate seating area adjacent to the pool was fitted with a custom fire bowl to allow for evening relaxation under the stars. With both an upper patio space and lower patio space, the alfresco areas could accommodate both large and intimate gatherings.

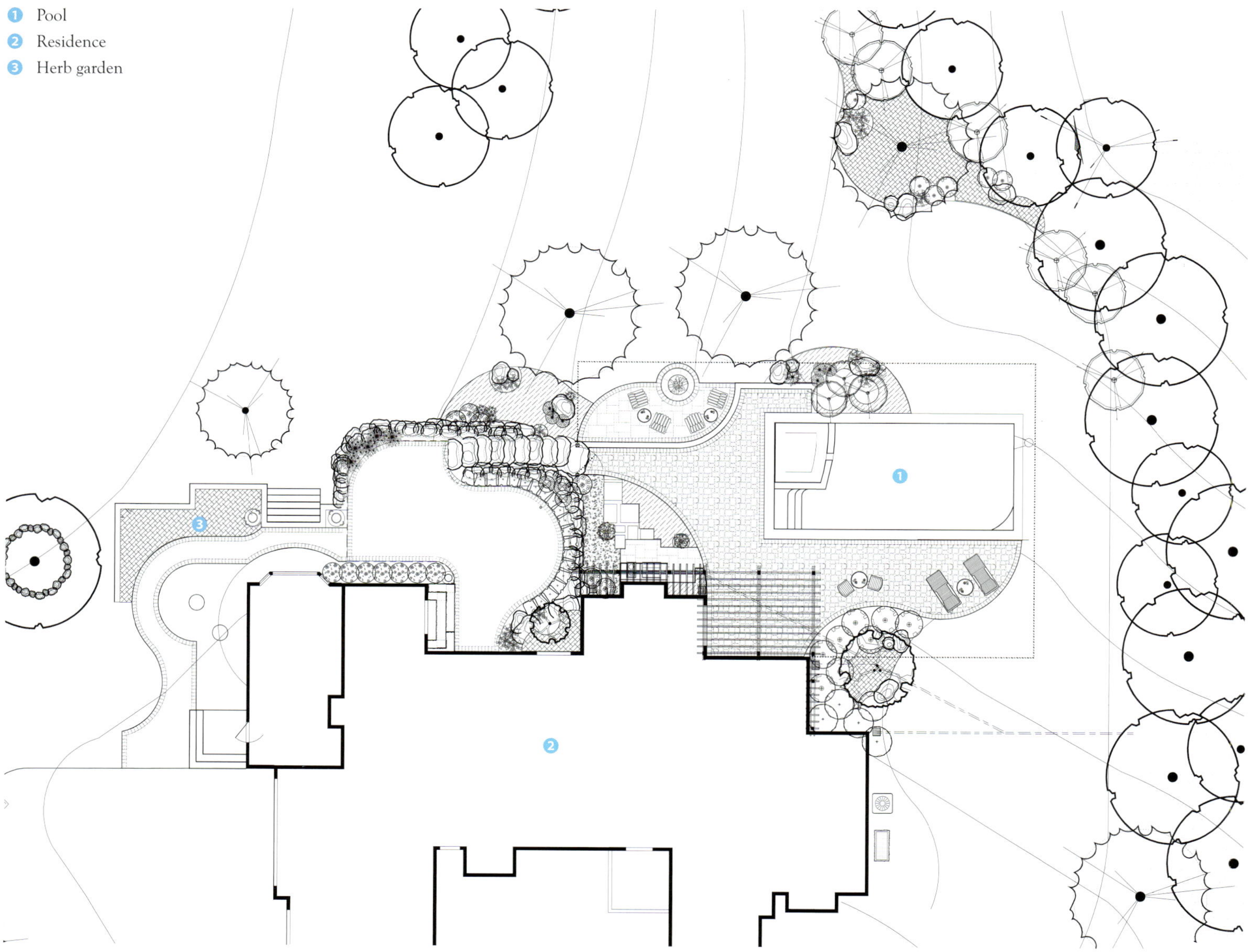

Site plan

Large stone outcrops were used to retain and establish the outdoor living areas and were softened with perennials and ground covers. The spa and pool were constructed with gunite, and limestone defined their edge. After dark, the outdoor space could be illuminated with low-voltage landscape lighting.

Arboretum Landmark Garden

Robert Edson Swain, Inc.

Seattle, United States

26,160 square feet (2430 square meters)

Photography / Andrew Ryznar, Robert Edson Swain, Inc

Containing one of the most diverse and important plant collections in North America, The Arboretum is internationally renowned for its collection of oaks, conifers, camellias, Japanese maples, and hollies. This landmark residence of enormous scale at 26,160 square feet (2430 square meters) offers a luxurious modernity merged perfectly with its historic character—the grounds are an extension of the arboretum and honor the legacy of the Olmsted greenbelt, while blending a European and Asian garden evolution. Great care was taken to pair the stone building with light and airy settings that create connections from the interior to the beautiful garden.

Stately Douglas fir and western redcedar were planted in the northern, shadier part of the garden, obstructing a view of the neighbors, allowing the home to be a part of the forest. This northwestern structure is softened with native sword ferns, *Vancouveria hexandra*, *Longleaf Mahonia* and exotic rhododendrons. A thunderous water feature pleasantly screens noise from the arterial road, with beautiful lady ferns, chain ferns, and bunchberry thriving around it.

The garden respects native northwest forestry while engaging the diversity of Arboretum collections, resulting in a fusion of East and West influences.

Master plan

Pop-up garden

Nicola Spinetto Architectes

Chiavari, Italy

2,013 square feet (187 square meters)

Photography / Sergio Grazia

The project transformed a neglected backyard into a multi-layered landscape garden. Designed for a private client in the Italian town of Chiavari, the pop-up garden gave new life to a steep outdoor area to provide natural terraces made from untreated Douglas fir, a shaded eating area, a small kitchen with an oven, and a deck for the family to enjoy.

Terraced garden plan

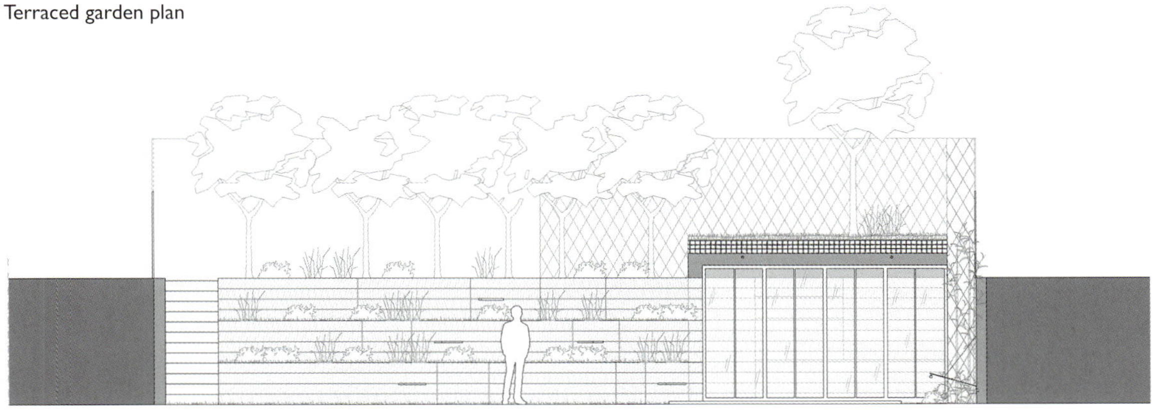

The concept for the project was based on the site's specific needs, which were in dealing with a 9-foot (3-meter) ground-level difference and the preservation of classified trees—leading to the idea of a terraced garden. Within these constraints, the project unfurled like a game, with curves and lines circumventing the existing landscape elements.

Additionally, the project sought to create a connection between the upper and lower parts of the garden within this volumetric treatment. The aesthetic is a result of a balance between those two parts: the old and preserved garden, which interacts with the new one below.

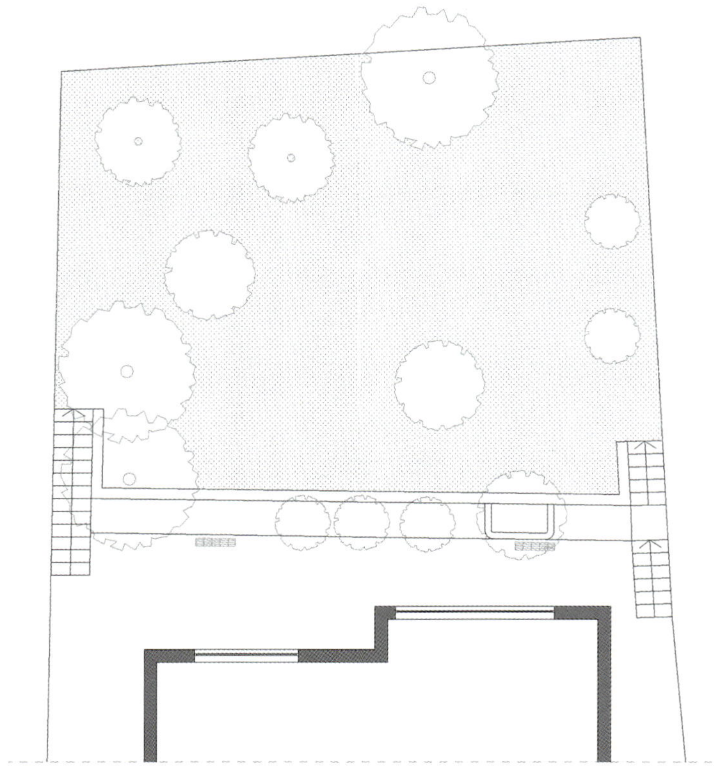

Existing plan

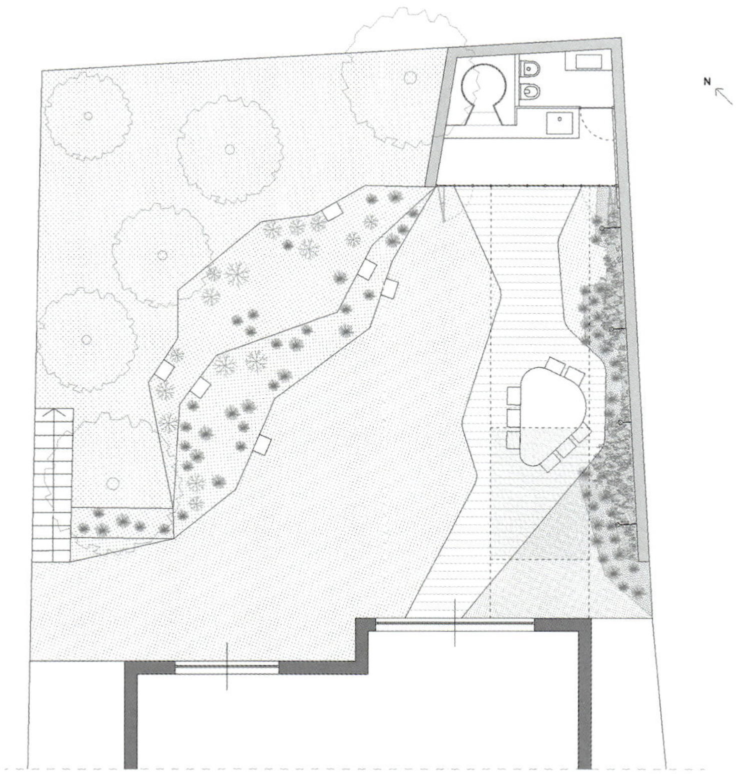

Project plan

Private Garden

Ethan McGory, Oakland Design Associates

Columbus, United States
23,681 square feet (2200 square meters)

Photography / Ethan McGory

The concept for this garden was to create a series of garden rooms to surround a large home with many views in and out. As the front of the home faces a corner and was fairly open to the street, a hedge of boxwood was extended across the front of the garden to separate the garden from the street and create a sense of cohesion through the front of the project.

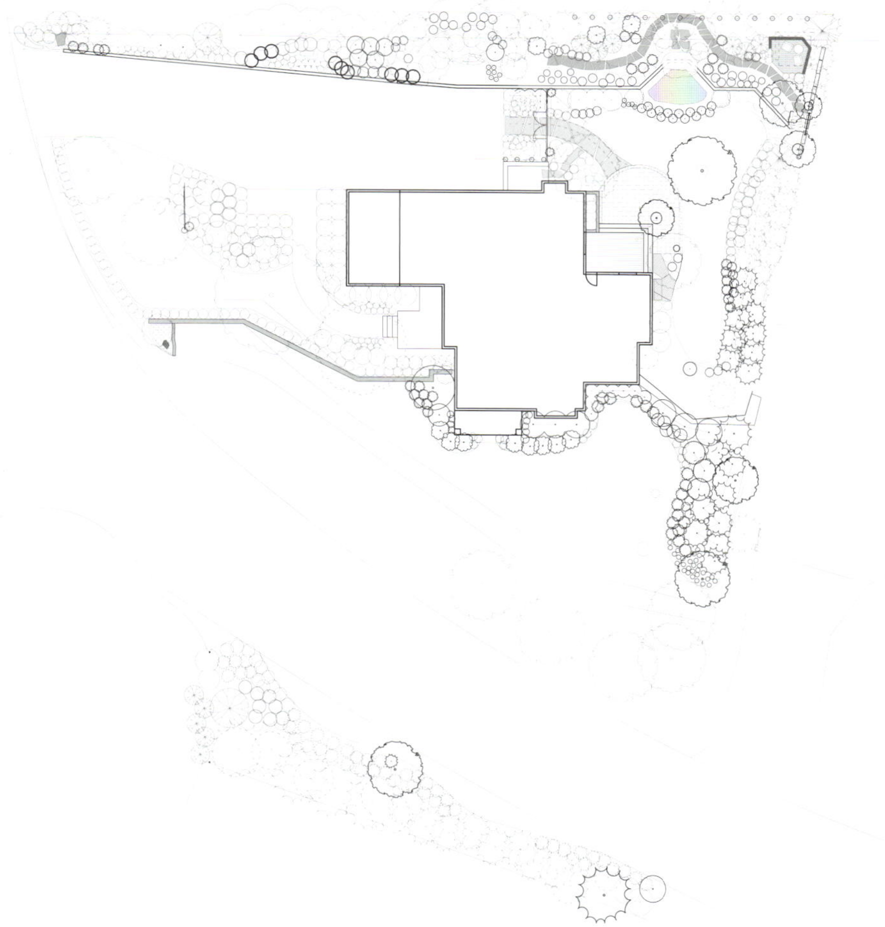

Site plan

The beds were tightly shaped, but full of the mixes of silvers, greens, whites, and purples. The color contrast was made to be relatively low in order to highlight differences in form and texture. Across the road from the entrance to the home, a mixture of evergreens and grasses were planted to improve views from the home and create more cohesion across the road.

The entrance to the backyard is through a gate planted with vines and flowering shrubs and trees. The gate screens the view from the street and creates a greater sense of arrival in the backyard. The backyard is centered around a low deck that steps down to a circular patio in the center of the yards.

The southern edge of the garden was hedged with evergreens, hostas, and ferns to create privacy from a nearby neighbor. The eastern edge of the garden was raised above the rest of the garden and sits on a retaining wall. In the center of the wall, a fountain cascades down into the lower portion of the garden.

Thatched cottage on the Schlei

Bahl GmbH

Ulsnis, Schleswig-Holstein, Germany
32,292 square feet (3000 square meters)

Planning office / Sebastian Jensen Hamburg
Photography / Miquel Tres

If you invest time in caring for your garden, you will have a more enjoyable space—especially when your garden captures views over the wider fields of Schleswig-Holstein and the waters of the nearby Schlei.

The wide sky, the proximity to the water, and an old farmhouse attracted the owners to the north of Germany, who decided to live permanently in a region where others only get to spend their holidays. When they bought the property, the garden was still a wilderness, which was taken into account as part of the redesign and divided in various garden spaces around the L-shaped building.

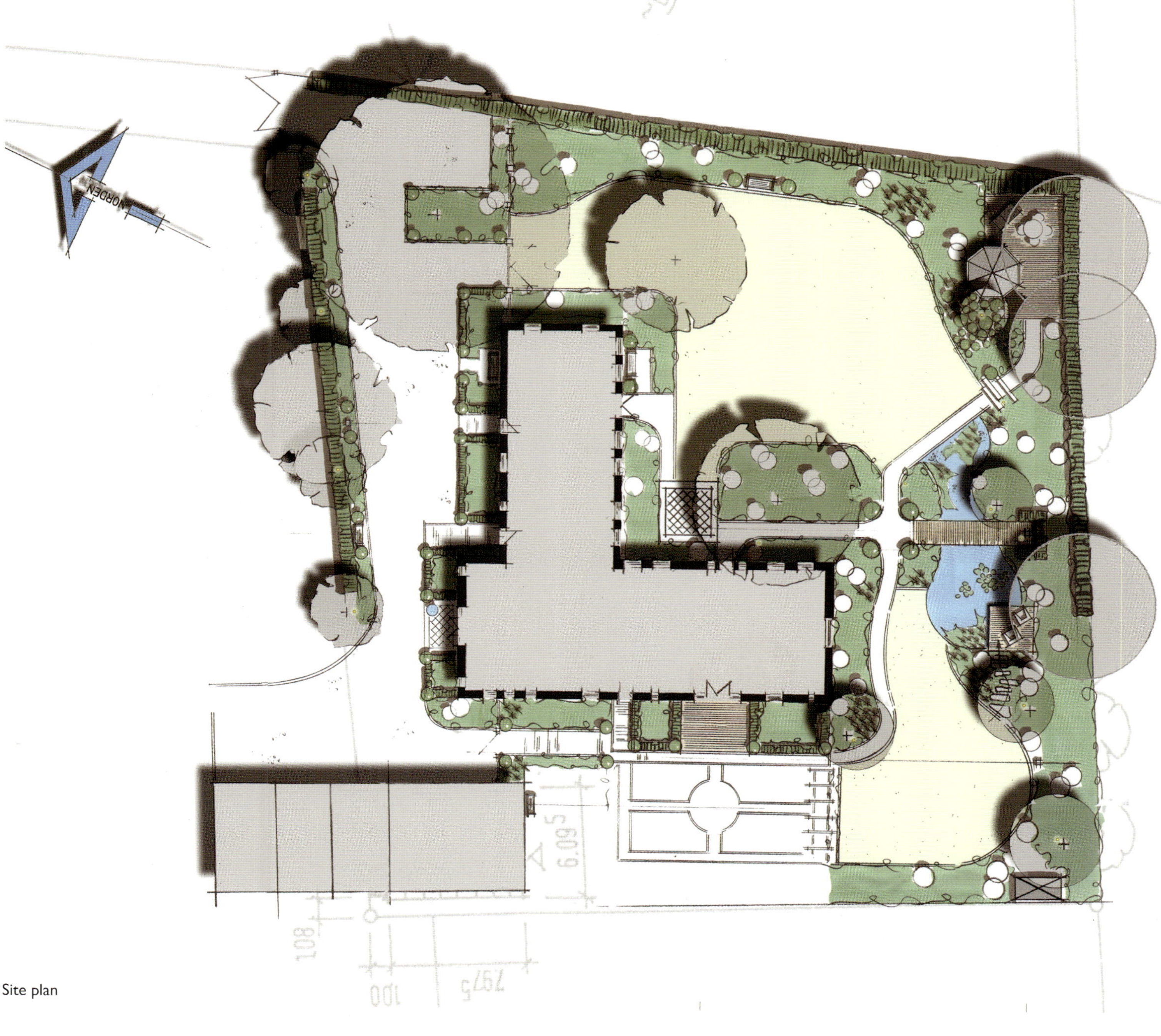

Site plan

The result was a cottage garden with roses, herbs, and fruit bushes, framed by low boxwood hedges. The existing pond was enlarged and upgraded with a dock and wooden deck, which created another seating area. A white lacquered teahouse on a rise in a corner of the property allows a view across the nearby landscape. Thanks to good planning, many seats allow never-ending new perspectives: in garden areas, at the lovingly restored house, the teahouse, and the pond. Foundry stone walls are typical for the region and worked to create a nice boundary.

In every season something blooms in this natural garden: in the spring daffodils and rhododendrons; in summer the numerous roses; and in the autumn asters, which conclude the garden's year with the grasses and the colorful foliage. Existing large trees—including an old apple tree, chestnut, plum, and cherry—were supplemented by large rock pears and fan maple. Targeted spotlights illuminate the trees, as well as stones and the teahouse after sunset.

Pacific Rim

Jeffrey Gordon Smith

Arroyo Grande, United States
17,600 square feet (1635 square meters)
Photography / Chris Leschinsky

This residence sits on the Nipomo Mesa high above expansive farm fields overlooking rolling dunes and the Pacific Ocean. The client's primary requests were a traditional Japanese garden and a deck off the back of the remodeled residence.

With such stunning views, it was easy to utilize the Japanese garden element of the "borrowed landscape" as the driving force of the design. Abstracting the quilt work of the farm fields beyond, Ipe hardwood deck boards alternate patterns while raised concrete planters house succulents planted to mimic crop rows, adding a modern twist to the traditional Japanese garden.

The farms below produce cut flowers and red leaf lettuce that tie in with the vibrant punch of the recycled magenta glass fire pit and raised bed of *Echeveria*. Beyond the deck, flowing drifts of mostly native plants emulate the soft curvature of the distant dunes.

Plant plan

Bloor West Garden

Janet Rosenberg & Studio

Toronto, Canada

7770 square feet (722 square meters)

Photography / Jeff McNeill Photography

The use of a simple palette of materials and clean architectural lines transformed this space into an elegant and relaxing outdoor retreat. Elements including a fireplace, a water feature, and a dining pavilion—with retractable panels for shade—organized the garden into a series of functional and beautiful spaces. The architectural constructions—namely the pavilion and fireplace—alluded to symbols of the hearth and the equivalence between interior and exterior as the unified cherished environment of the homestead. Key to the dynamism of the design was the contrast between the orthogonal entropy of the enclosure with the centripetal extropy of the landscape.

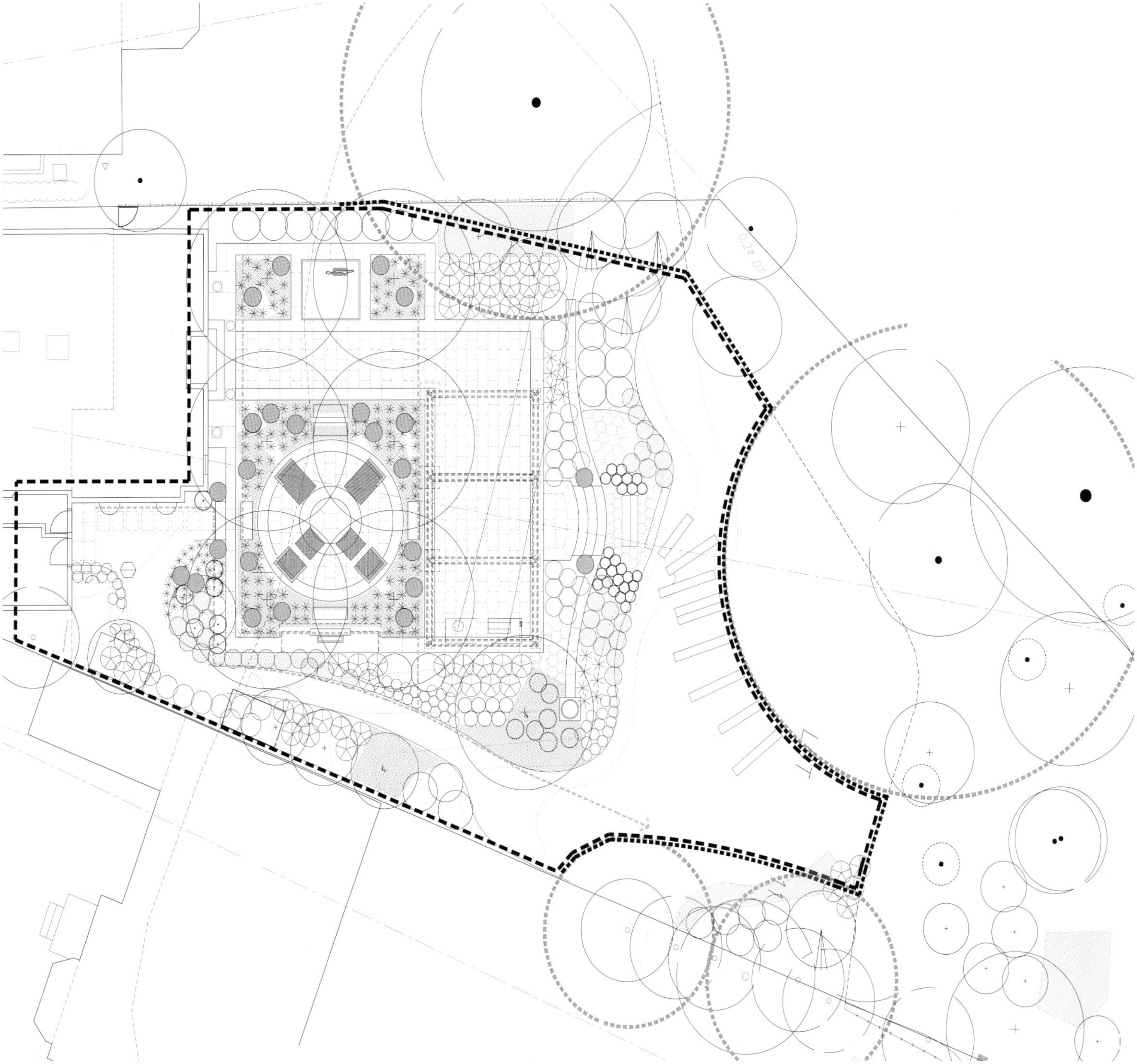

Site plan

From the upper stone terrace the garden cascades gracefully to a small stone terrace, surrounded by the natural beauty of Grenadier Pond beyond. The view of it below creates the destination within the stepped sequence of openness in the garden spaces. This view also reveals the sheltering effect of the perimeter trees, further defining landscape elements as important as architectural constructs in shaping the experience of the exterior living room.

The stairs were interpreted as the medium of transition between enclosed, sheltered and the open landscape environments. Beyond, the stepping stones—which were expressed in the same dimensions—appear to dissolve from the stair embankment, simulating the terraced spaces as nested islands within the greater landscape. Further separation through planting as "parterres de pelouse" reinforces the sense of rooms within the greater whole, as well as inviting the future layering, which trees create as canopy or ceiling. In addition, symmetry in the planting reinforces the metaphor of the inside outside.

Noteworthy too is the abstracted pond of rippling water jets that not only echoes the presence of Grenadier Pond, but also metaphorically represents the varied nodes of activity across the garden. In this way, this built pond creates a simulation of the sight and sound beyond, capitalizing on the nature and privileges of the site.

Private garden in Fockbek

Bahl GmbH

Fockbek, Schleswig-Holstein, Germany
15,069 square feet (1400 square meters)

Planning office / Sebastian Jensen Hamburg
Photography / Miquel Tres

The owner's passion for the garden started after the house was built, as they wanted an outdoor environment that would connect with the building. Having a space to escape from the frenzy of life at the end of the day. As such, the designs sought to create zones for relaxation.

The layout of the seats, walkways, and hedges were oriented on the lines of the house. Black granite slabs lead to a lowered seating area with aluminum and wood furniture, with yew balls (*Taxus baccata*) completing

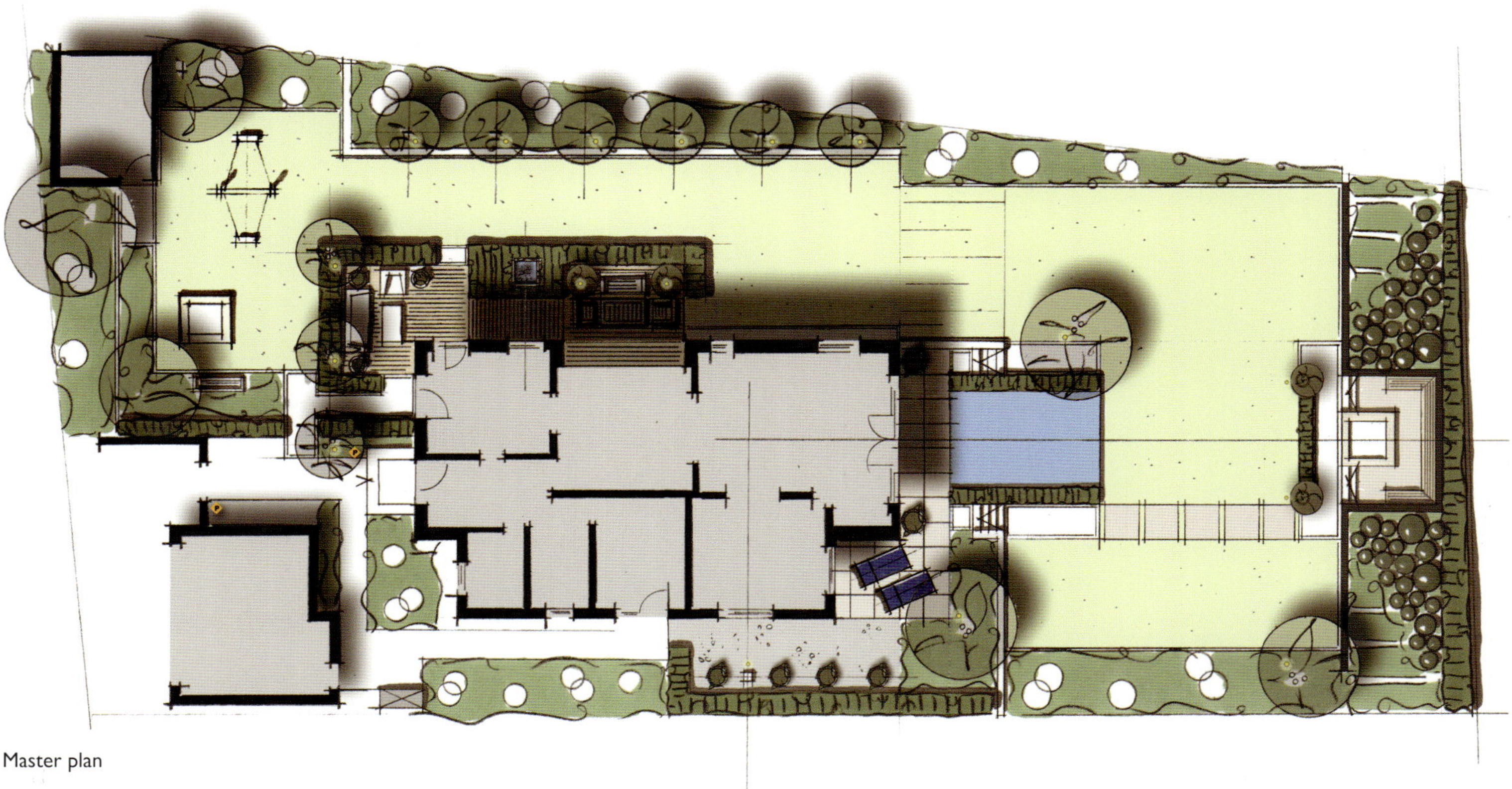

Master plan

the area. In the vicinity of the house, tables and chairs made of larch wood invite visitors to linger.

Attractive points of view—such as the seven high-stemmed column hain beeches with tapered tree tops and the two slit-thorn trees in Domani planters at the lowered seating area—provide optical highlights. In the spring, rhododendron and azaleas bloom; in the summer, the perennials and hydrangeas blossom with beautiful white, pink, and violet colors accenting the evergreen plants. This was particularly important to the owners, as the joy of the garden can also be experienced in winter.

Private space in Boucherville

Art & Jardins Conception

Boucherville, Canada

53,820 square feet (5000 square meters)

Photography / Jean-Claude Hurni

On the banks of the St. Lawrence River at the end of a road is a vast house of stone with large wooden doors. In front, in a harmonious extension, the linear pedestrian entrance presents as a garden in itself. The driveway is spacious and the stone that composes it gives it a beautiful nobility that combines well with that of the house.

Alignments of shrubs with evergreen foliage and conifers helped to structure this garden to make it very present in all seasons. These simple lines were well encompassed with flowering plants with a flexible and generous design. With its well-constructed character and its graceful appearance, the front garden added to the beauty of the residence.

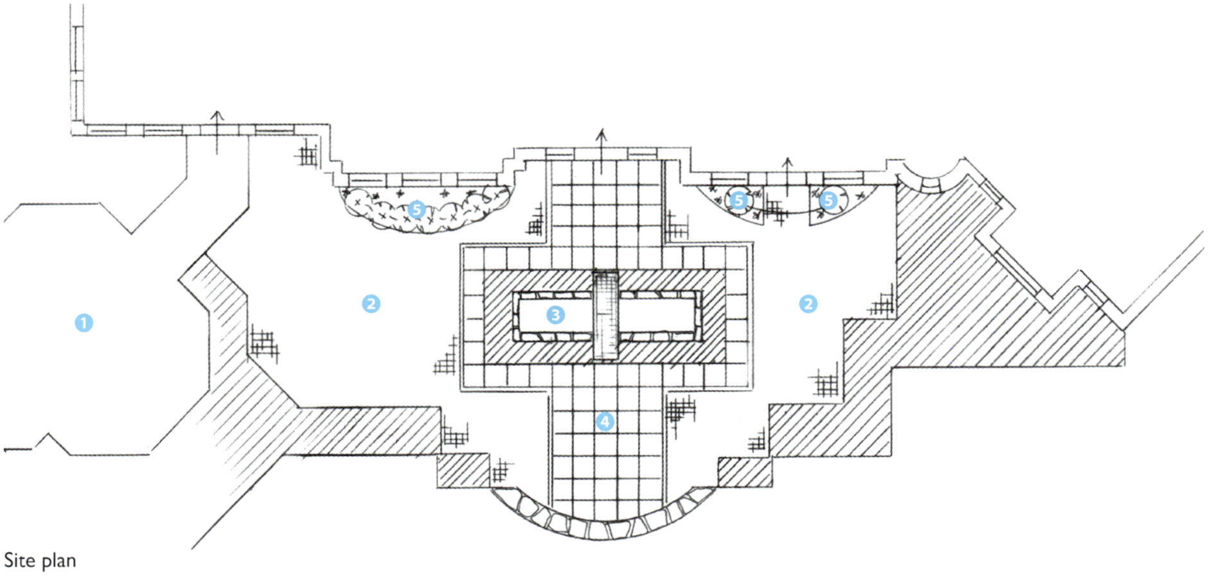

1 Solarium
2 Existing paving
3 Basin
4 Stones
5 Boxwood

Site plan

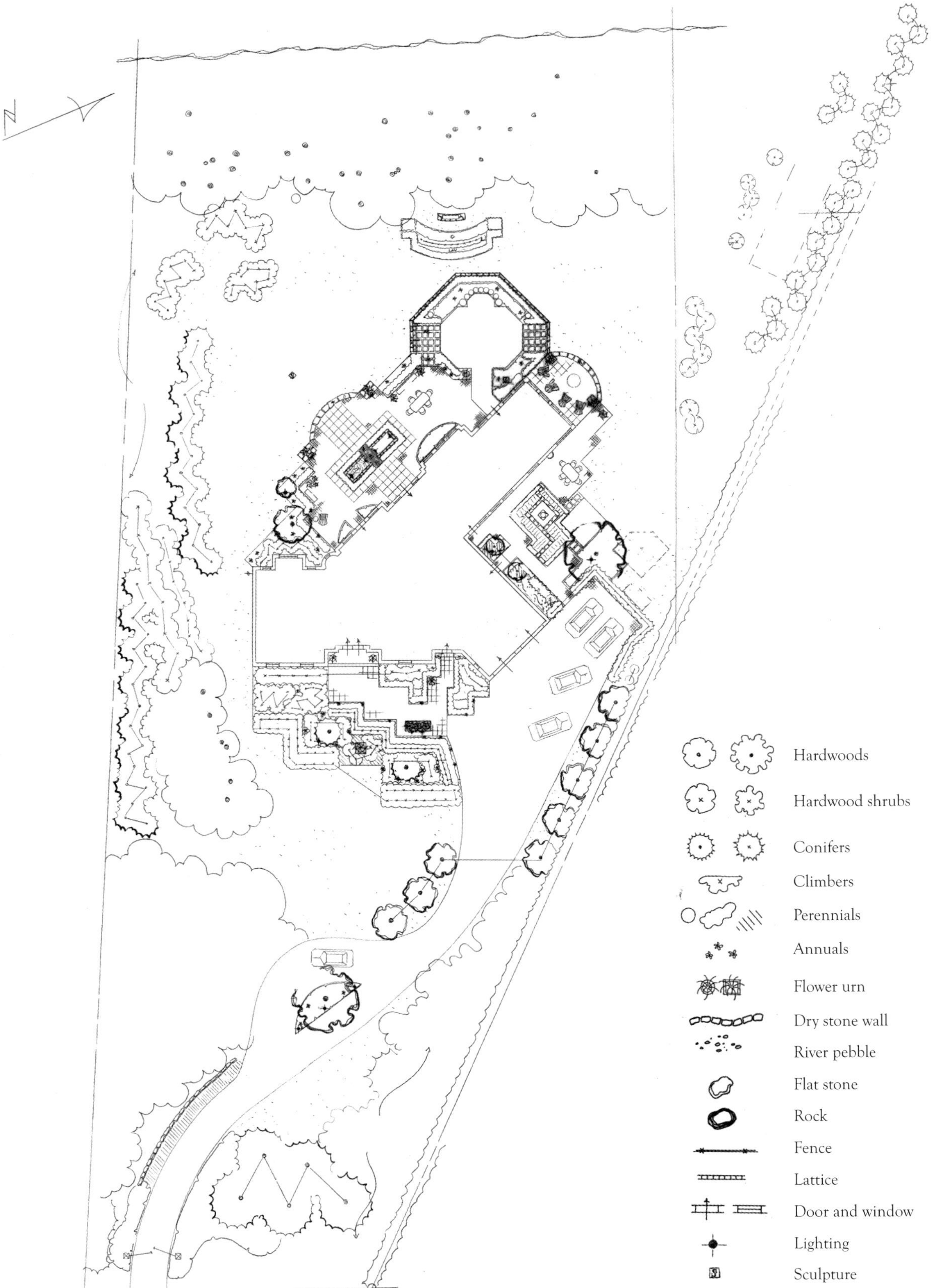

Hardwoods
Hardwood shrubs
Conifers
Climbers
Perennials
Annuals
Flower urn
Dry stone wall
River pebble
Flat stone
Rock
Fence
Lattice
Door and window
Lighting
Sculpture

Site plan

Everywhere on the ground surrounding this monumental building, grace and strength come together to marry in a very elegant way. The height of the spruce and the volume of the spireas give a calmness and pleasure to the whole while the pieces of ornament judiciously chosen and well-arranged here and there catch the eyes. The long classical pool was intended to be an important point of the garden, with its metal grid serving as a bridge linking two sections of the same large patio.

On the river side, where the horizon is the law, a natural setting was created from scratch to escape the neighborhood while maintaining a magnificent view of this large body of water that fits into the décor. Thuya hedges, abundant vegetation, and large patios make it possible to create private gathering areas, as desired by the owners, who wanted a space to host both intimate family gatherings as well as larger groups of guests.

Garden with the water channel

Atelier Flera

Rychnov, Czech Republic
13,778 square feet (1280 square meters)

Photography / Atelier Flera

Located in Rychnov, Czech Republic, this garden by Atelier Flera transformed an existing space. Starting with the lawn, existing shrubs and trees were removed and the Siberian larch beams were placed in a trench, which, together with the gravel, serve as a footpath around the house. Some of the beams of the sidewalk were finished with vertical beams with recessed lighting, which was slightly embedded in the hedge. Everything was supplemented with saplings and distinctive blue, white, and cream tones.

The slope next to the entrance was divided into two elevation levels with an inserted birch flowerpot, which was situated there due to the presence of utility networks in this part of the plot. To the left of the access road were constructed wooden stairs, ending with a gate and a fence. The water element in the garden was preexisting from the previous design. The designer simply widened the terrace to better fit the dining table and chairs.Main vegetation adjustments were made on the main residential part of the garden. They added two more to the existing Tartar maple and unified plantations of undergrowth, mostly perennials and grasses.

Vegetation adjustments were made on the main residential part of the garden. They added two more to the existing Tatar maple and unified plantations of undergrowth, mostly perennials and grasses. A pergola was added to complement the shield from the neighbor, and the concrete washed pavement was replaced for a smoother alternative, both outside and in the indoor pool area.

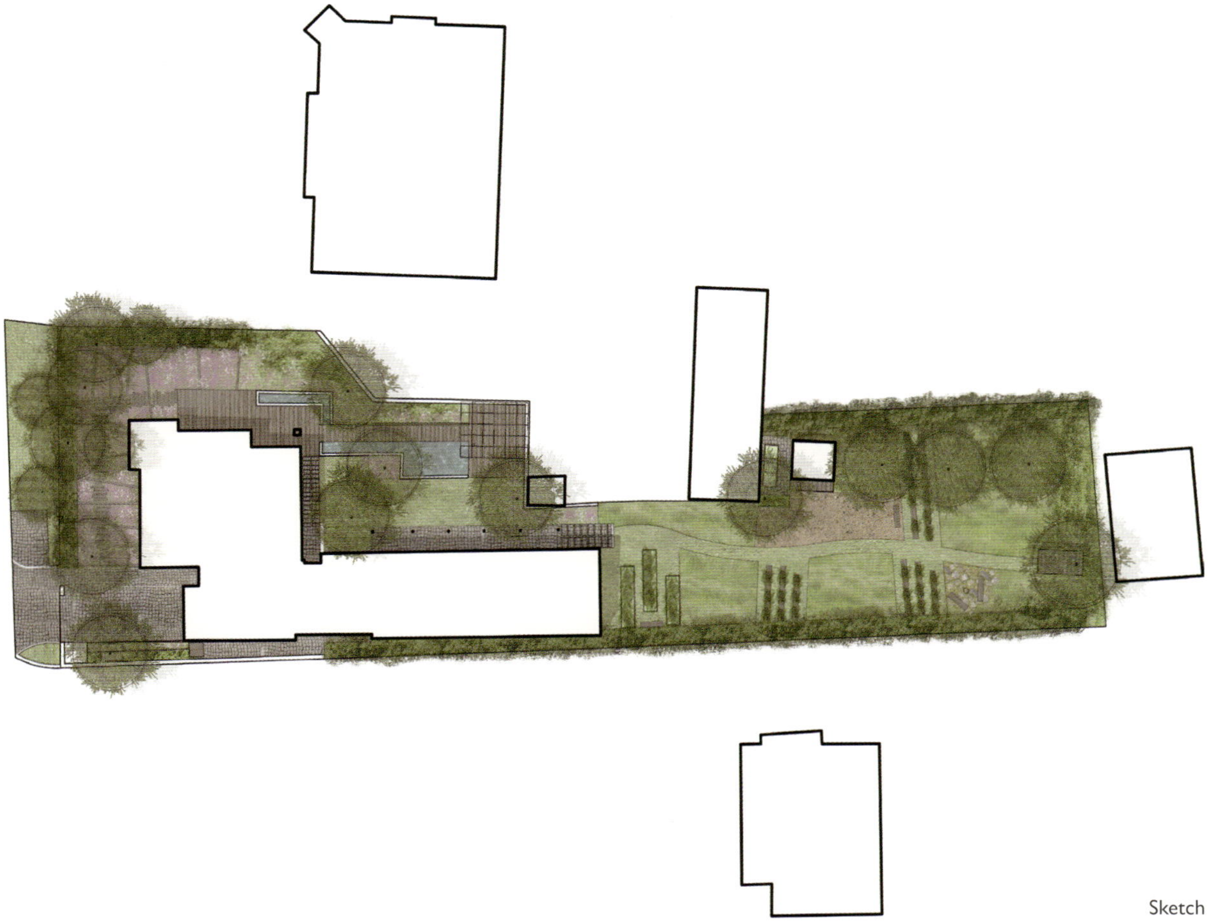

Sketch

From the gates, a series of features become prominent—a cubby in the walnut tree, a fireplace area, three elevated vegetable beds with a bench, a pétanque, garden house, and a small vineyard on both sides of the road, along with a meadow, which complements the traditional element of a Czech garden.

Index

A. J. Miller Landscape Architecture P076—www.ajmillerla.com, mmiller@ajmillerla.com

Art & Jardins Conception PP046, 060, 146, 176, 232—www.artetjardins.net, info@artetjardins.net

Atelier Flera PP034, 070, 238—www.flera.cz, atelier@flera.cz

Bahl GmbH PP022, 040, 054, 210, 228—www.bahl-gaerten.de, info@bahl-gaerten.de

David Keegan Garden Design P084—www.dkgardendesign.co.uk, info@dkgardendesign.co.uk

Design Focus International PP096, 140—www.designfocus.com, contact@designfocus.com

Erik van Gelder P108—www.erikvangelder.com, info@erikvangelder.com

Ethan McGory P206—www.ethanmcgory.com, gardens@ethanmcgory.com

Guz Architects PP102, 184—www.guzarchitects.com, guz@guzarchitects.com

Jailmake Ltd P154—www.jailmake.com, studio@jailmake.com

Janet Rosenberg & Studio PP028, 128, 222—www.jrstudio.ca, office@jrstudio.ca

Jeffrey Gordon Smith P218—www.jgsdesigns.com

Lotus Design Studio P064—www.lotusdesignstudio.co.uk, info@lotusdesignstudio.co.uk

Lynne Marcus Garden and Landscape Design PP122, 134—www.lynnemarcus.co.uk, gardendesign@lynnemarcus.com

Nicola Spinetto Architectes P200—www.nicolaspinetto.com, ns@nicolaspinetto.com

Robert Edson Swain, Inc. PP090, 168, 192—www.robertedsonswain.com, bob@bobswain.com

R. Youngblood & Co. PP016, 116, 162, 188—www.ryoungblood.com, info@ryoungblood.com